The Political Economy
of the Black Ghetto

The Political
Economy of the
Black Ghetto

William K. Tabb

THE UNIVERSITY OF CONNECTICUT

W · W · NORTON & COMPANY · INC ·

NEW YORK

Contents

Preface

The title of this book promises a study in "political economy." By this term the author seeks to place his work in the tradition of those who think of economics as the study of men in their roles as producers and consumers in a social setting. Thus the black ghetto is studied as an economic unit which is part of a larger society. The purpose of this work is to describe the economic factors which help explain the origins of the black ghetto, and the mechanisms through which exploitation and deprivation are perpetuated; and to explore strategies for ending them.

In the emotional discussion of race it is too easily forgotten that the same economic laws operate in this area as elsewhere. The systematic racism so often described cannot be effectively fought by merely denouncing bigotry and calling for more legislation: the important enemies are not the crude bigots, and there are already too many laws which are not being enforced. Racism is perpetuated by elements of oppression within an economic and political system which must be understood *as a system*. The present study attempts to isolate key elements which can help us understand the historic role of blacks in the American economy and the nature of contemporary white-black relations. Not a systematic study of capitalism—it examines the *impact* of contemporary capitalism on the black ghetto.

I am grateful to Matthew Edel of M.I.T. and to my colleagues at the University of Connecticut, Harold Abramson, Larry Carney, Robert Reilly, Robert N. Schoeplein, James Scully, Stephen Q. Welch, and H. John Thorkelson for reading and commenting on parts of the manuscript. I am also indebted to students taking part in the University's Urban Semester Program and participants in the Inter-racial Leadership Training Program, and their very able director, the Reverend Jack Allen, as well as the students of my urban economics classes, on whom much of this material was first tried. More than a few of their ideas have been incorporated. Mrs. Betty G. Seaver typed a flawless manuscript, earning my sincerest gratitude. Arthur J. Malloy, my research assistant, gathered much of the data for the study.

I am also indebted to two former teachers, William Appleman Williams and Harvey Goldberg of the University of Wisconsin. Their modes of analysis and incisive thinking cannot but continue to affect a student many years after he has left their classrooms. I have benefited, too, from long hours of heated but always educational debate with Richard H. Day, also of the University of Wisconsin.

Material presented in this book draws on previously published studies, including a paper presented to a conference at the University of Hartford, November 15, 1969, which appears in *Explorations in Urban Land Economics*, edited by John J. Sullivan, John C. Lincoln Institute; and from material which has appeared in the *Journal of Economic Issues* and *Land Economics*. I am grateful for the opportunity to make use of these studies in this book.

W. K. T.

CHAPTER 1

Themes, Methodology, and an Example

Survey after survey shows Americans continuing to believe that ghetto unrest, riots, and rebellion are caused by criminals, outside agitators, and "foreign" communist influences. The level of political debate over the need for more "law and order" indicates the lack of understanding of economic and social causality.

On the other hand, research findings consistently demonstrate the presence of discrimination against blacks in education, jobs, and housing. Racism pervades every institution in America from churches to universities. Many scholars have studied in depth one or more of these manifestations and have suggested reforms of different sorts.

We are here concerned with the motivations for institutional racism, with how labor markets and housing markets, governments and unions, affect the lives of black Americans. There are those who believe that "white perceptions of Negroes, and the historical inculcation of these perceptions in the minds of Negroes themselves, are at the root of our present troubles."[1] Unquestionably individual racism, with its dehumanizing effects on both blacks and

[1] Senator Fred R. Harris, Foreword, in William H. Grier and Price M. Cobbs, *Black Rage* (New York: Bantam, 1968), p. viii.

1

whites, is important. It is individual racists who perpetuate the institutions which deny equal rights to blacks and other minority groups. But individual racism is not solely responsible: we must work not only to cure the hearts and minds of men. Men are shaped by their upbringing, by the institutional environment in which they mature. Institutional change is therefore desirable which brings immediate gain for blacks while contributing to the long-run elimination of racism. Attitudes are often formed and ideologies constructed to fulfill the selfish interests of individuals and groups. These attitudes may take on a life of their own, but they are creatures spawned of special needs. As Grier and Cobbs have written: "Slavery required the creation of a particular kind of person, one *compatible* with a life of involuntary servitude. The ideal slave had to be absolutely dependent and have a deep consciousness of personal inferiority. . . . Teachings so painstakingly applied do not disappear easily."[2] And of course the white man had to justify the place of the slave—he was a child who had to be cared for. The attitude continues down to the present day. "A modern version holds that black people are little different from other citizens save for a paucity of education and money. The reason for these deficiencies is left vague."[3] Yet the reasons are not vague. The task is to question attitudes formed; how economics, social relations and personality development interact.

Since the economics profession has turned its collective back on the tradition of approaching social relations and ideological norms from the political economist's vantage point, the present study may be described as "interdisciplinary." However, the models developed and the approach taken are in the nineteenth-century tradition of political economy as practiced by Ricardo, Mill and Marx.

One major theme in the following pages can be put in either positive or negative terms. Negatively: Poverty and urban-development programs will not succeed as long as they are based on an incorrect understanding of the place of black people and the black ghetto in the economy of the United States. More positively: Success in changing the living conditions in the ghetto necessitates the rupture of the colonial relationship which now exists between

[2] Grier and Cobbs, *Black Rage*, pp. 20–21.
[3] *Ibid.*, p. 21.

the ghetto and the larger society. "The dark ghettos," as Kenneth Clark has written, "are social, political, educational, and—above all—economic colonies. Their inhabitants are subject peoples, victims of the greed, cruelty, insensitivity, guilt, and fear of their masters."[4] The economic relation is a key one in understanding the ghetto. It has been the most ignored in studies to date.

A second theme is the interplay between polar approaches to change: integration-separatism, white domination-black liberation, and evolution-revolution. These dichotomies will be undercurrents in much of what is said. For example, such questions as whether white businesses should be given subsidies to invest in the ghetto, or black capitalism should be encouraged, cannot be answered simply in terms of applying conventional economic analysis— marginalism, cost-benefit analysis, and so forth. Individual viewpoints dictate the crucial assumptions which strongly influence, if not predetermine, the outcome of subsequent analysis.

The approach of analyzing the black ghetto as a colony of white society—an interpretation increasingly in vogue with militant blacks and some academics, denied vociferously by (among others) most moderates and liberal politicians—is a useful one. It allows the application to the ghetto of theoretic tools of analysis used in the study of developing nations. It has its limitations, but it offers a most useful organizing framework which has been absent in many previous discussions. The ghetto as colony is the subject of Chapter 2.

Chapter 3 considers why blacks do not own the economic resources of the ghetto and discusses the relevance of proposals for "black capitalism." Incentives to private industry for locating in the ghetto are given a separate chapter (4), in which the limits of the options open to the ghetto within the market system are made more clearly visible. Chapter 5 views welfare as being imposed and perpetuated upon the ghetto by white society. It explores why this is so, and how the policy is sustained. Consideration is given in Chapter 6 to ways in which the labor market fosters colonial relationships.

The concluding chapter discusses alternative proposals for re-

[4] Kenneth B. Clark, *Dark Ghetto: Dilemmas of Social Power* (New York: Harper Torchbooks, 1967), p. 11.

building the ghetto and American society. The rhetorical promise of the commonly enunciated long-range goals can be contrasted with both the absence of commitment to achieve those goals and a lack of understanding of how they can be achieved. The naïveté of traditional liberal analysis, by obscuring power relations, impedes progress. Fundamental change must be based on a clear analysis of socio-economic forces.

The book as a whole is both descriptive and analytic in approach. How things work and why things are as they are—these are our concerns. Facts that shock when first learned have a way of becoming all too comfortably accepted over time. Reforms that fail lead to defeatist attitudes. Understanding socio-economic relations, on the other hand, leads to a more realistic assessment of what causes problems and which types of solutions make sense. Major problems we encounter at the outset are false awareness of causation and denial of important social problems (like the existence of racism and exploitation), matters worth discussing briefly.

Subjective Comprehension and Objective Reality

The relation between objective conditions and subjective understanding of these conditions involves a complex and continuing interaction. Our perception of reality changes the objective nature of that reality. As objective conditions change, our subjective interpretation of the world around us changes. The relation is never in a one-to-one correspondence. Subjective judgments may lag behind objective reality, and always judgment is tempered by past thinking, by education, by the social role of the observer, and by his own self-interest. So it is in our thinking about the position of blacks in American society. Objective judgment is made difficult by white feelings of guilt, hatred, and fear, mixed with denial of wrongs and appeal to the substantial nature of the progress already made. Thus "progress," "reform," and "improvement," on the one hand, and "worsening conditions," "crisis proportions," and "deprivation," on the other, are used to describe the same basic data. Consider the following statement from a 1967 government study: "The incidence of poverty among nonwhite families remains high, with about one out of three classified as poor. Still, just six years ago one out of two of the nonwhite families were poor."[5] The seriousness of poverty among blacks depends on one's viewpoint. Things are getting better. Things are still pretty bad. If one is not personally suffering, it is easier to think of progress made and how impressive it has been. However, the black rebellion underscores for whites the fact that the destiny of this country is tied to the way it deals with the race question.

Just before Richard Nixon was inaugurated president, his counselor Daniel P. Moynihan gave him a "Memorandum for the President on the Position of Negroes."[6] The memorandum offered the president the following advice: "The Negro lower class must be dissolved by transforming it into a stable working class population." It is "the low-income marginally employed, poorly educated, disorganized slum dwellers" whom "black extremists use to threaten white society with the prospects of mass arson and pillage." Therefore, says Moynihan, these people must be turned into "truck drivers, mail carriers, assembly line workers—people with dignity, purpose, and in the United States, a very good standard of living indeed." Mr. Moynihan might have also noted that the real wages of factory workers have gone down over the last four years because their money wages have increased less than the prices of the goods they buy. As to the mail carriers, the unresponsiveness of Congress to their needs has caused this group of workers to feel so put upon as to stage wildcat strikes, tying up mail for days in such important cities as New York and Chicago. It is also of interest to note that the one industry in which the Nixon Administration has pursued a policy of gently forcing the hiring of more blacks is the construction industry—one of the sectors of the economy experiencing unemployment of increasingly important proportions at the time the Administration was pushing the so-called

[5] U.S. Department of Labor, Bureau of Labor Statistics; and U.S. Department of Commerce, Bureau of the Census, *Social and Economic Conditions of Negroes in the United States* (Washington, D.C.: Government Printing Office, 1967), p. ix.

[6] " '69 Moynihan Memo to President Urged Jobs for Negroes," *The New York Times*, March 1, 1970, p. 1, and "Text of Memorandum for the President, by Daniel P. Moynihan, counselor to President Nixon, on the position of Negroes," *ibid.*, p. 69. Subsequent quotations before the next note reference are taken from this memorandum.

Philadelphia Plan. Insensitivity to such factors may be costly to all concerned, and optimistic statistics may disguise severe underlying social tensions. Mr. Moynihan stressed the progress made: "Young Negro families are achieving income parity with young white families. Outside the South, young husband-wife Negro families have 99 percent of the income of the whites! . . . Thus, it may be this ancient gap is finally closing."

While Moynihan did mention the increase in the number of poor black children in female-headed families (these were 2,241,000 such children in 1968 as against only 1,947,000 in male-headed families), the picture he presented was essentially optimistic.

He gathered from the evidence that "The time may have come when the issue of race could benefit from a period of 'benign neglect.' The subject is too much talked about. . . . We may need a period in which Negro progress continues and racial rhetoric fades." He talked about giving more recognition to the moderates, the "silent black majority" and went as far as to appoint it a leader: "I would take it, for example, that Ambassador [Jerome H.] Holland is a natural leader of this segment of the black community. There are others like him." Moynihan also suggested more research on crime.

The strategy expressed is fairly simple. To restore faith in self-regulating, gradual progress and the continuity of American institutions as we know them, we must strengthen the black middle class, set it up once again as a model to the rest of the black community. This, along with better police methods and isolating "extremists," is the best way of ending violent confrontations which lead to chaos. However, Moynihan's strategy also effectively polarizes the black community.

As Andrew Brimmer pointed out, the evidence can be interpreted to show that "within the Negro community, there appears to be a deepening schism between the able and less able, between the well-prepared and those with few skills."[7] For the latter group things are getting relatively worse and in some ways absolutely worse as well.

Brimmer saw a great deal of evidence for this view. The per-

[7] Andrew F. Brimmer, "Economic Progress of Negroes in the United States: The Deepening Schism," presented at the Founders' Day Convocation at Tuskegee Institute on March 22, 1970, mimeo.

centage of blacks in professional and technical occupations has risen, but so has the proportion in low-skilled occupations. There has been a drop in unemployment but an increase in the long-term unemployed. The increase in black family income compared to white has become greater, while the income of black families headed by women has declined.

In the last decade median nonwhite family income rose from 54 percent of white median family income in 1959 to 63 percent in 1968. However, said Brimmer, these statistics may be misleading. "It appears that in 1967 the median income data unadjusted for differences in family size may have overstated the relative economic status of nonwhite families by something on the order of 11 percent."[8] This miscalculation is due in part to the different average family size in the two surveys.

In addition, nonwhites have over the last decade accounted for a greater percentage of the poor. They were 27.9 percent of the total number of poor in 1959 and 31.5 percent in 1968. As more people get out of poverty, the percentage of nonwhite poor should continue to increase, because the typical black "poor" family is poorer than the typical white "poor" family—38.9 percent poorer in 1968. Thus, Brimmer argued that conditions were getting worse for significant numbers of blacks who were falling farther behind whites. This called for more, not less, assistance.

In answer to Moynihan, Brimmer said, "I am convinced that it would be a serious mistake to conclude that the black community has been so blessed with the benefits of economic advancement that public policy—which played such a vital role in the 1960s—need no longer treat poverty and deprivation among such a large segment of society as a matter of national concern. To accept such a view would certainly amount to neglect—but it would also be far from benign."[9]

Part of the black consciousness which has developed over the past decade has been the growth of a deeper sense of the type of society desired. The demand for jobs has been replaced by the demand for meaningful jobs, the demand for integrated education replaced by a concern for education controlled by the community

[8] *Ibid.*, p. 11.
[9] *Ibid.*, p. 3.

and geared to its own unique interests. The implications of such demands are immense. They call for nothing less than adopting a new rationale for social organization. The slogan "Serve the People" takes on a new and deeper meaning.

The Urban Context

There is ample reason to believe that the city will be the site of most aspects of the racial struggle in the years to come. Large numbers of blacks have moved off the land and into the cities, pushed by the general lack of any other employment opportunities and by the mechanization of Southern agriculture—as well as by the violence and intimidation encountered in the South, and drawn by the lure of jobs and the promise of opportunity in the North. In the foreseeable future, the black ghettos will continue to grow, abetted by perverse public policies. Projections for 1985 are for black majorities to populate many of our large cities: Chicago, Philadelphia, St. Louis, Detroit, Baltimore, New Orleans, Cleveland, even Richmond and Jacksonville. The nation's capital is already over 50 percent black. Such projections make any hope of integrated schools an impossibility for whole cities as it is now an impossibility for some black neighborhoods. In this light the demands for community control and ghetto enrichment become perhaps more realistic methods of raising educational standards than waiting for integration.

The increase in the number of blacks living in central cities can be seen in the following figures. In 1950 black people composed 13 percent of the population in cities of a million or more; in 1966 they were 26 percent of the total. In 1950, 6.5 million blacks lived in our central cities; in 1960, 9.7 million; and in 1966 12.1 million. The number of whites in the central cities decreased from 47.7 million to 46.4 million between 1960 and 1966. It is estimated that, at the time of this writing, there are 13.6 million blacks living in the central cities, and that by 1985 there will be 20.3 million. If there is no further net migration to the central cities, there will still be 17.3 million blacks living there in 1985.[10]

[10] The National Advisory Commission on Civil Disorders, *Report of the National Advisory Commission on Civil Disorders* (New York: Bantam, 1968), Chapter 6.

For most black Americans there has really not been much choice of where to live. Wherever they have lived, North or South, they have been isolated from the rest of society. As Gunnar Myrdal has reminded us, "Patterns of segregation developed as a part of the social heritage of Americans."[11]

The existence of segregation is one of the most obvious facts of American society. The hope that, with improvement in socio-economic status, residential segregation would decrease has not been borne out. The black population moving to our cities has not had the same experience as other immigrant groups. As the Taubers have written:

> In broad perspective, the historical trend toward improving socioeconomic status of immigrant groups has gone hand in hand with decreasing residential segregation. In contrast, Negro residential segregation from whites has increased steadily over past decades until it has reached universally high levels in cities throughout the United States, despite advances in the socioeconomic status of Negroes.[12]

For our black population, segregation has either remained at its high levels or increased still further. The nation's fifty largest central cities between 1950 and 1960 "without exception . . . regardless of their regional location, show increases in the proportion of nonwhite."[13] The twelve largest central cities in this period lost over two million whites while gaining 1.8 million nonwhites.[14]

The task before us is to understand what effects this increasing concentration will have and to design policies to end exploitation of blacks. While various official government reports view urban problems in relation to low income and racial discrimination, goals are still not clearly defined, and agency operations are ineffective.

Since neither goals nor priorities are clear, programs proliferate without any over-all plan of attack. The problems are the diversity

[11] Gunnar Myrdal, "National Planning for Healthy Cities: Two Challenges to Affluence," in *Planning for a Nation of Cities*, ed. Sam Bass Warner, Jr. (Cambridge, Mass.: The M.I.T. Press, 1966), p. 4.
[12] Karl E. Tauber and Alma F. Tauber, "The Negro As an Immigrant Group: Recent Trends in Racial and Ethnic Segregation in Chicago," *The American Journal of Sociology*, January, 1964, p. 378.
[13] Harry Sharp and Leo F. Schnore, "The Changing Color Composition of Metropolitan Areas," *Land Economics*, July 1962, p. 169.
[14] *Ibid.*, p. 174.

of goals and of clientele, and the conflict among objectives and among interest groups. In the clamorous discussion of the "Urban Crisis," three positions can be distinguished without doing violence to the multiplicity of viewpoints—those concerned with community, those concerned with the viability of the central city, and those concerned with race and poverty. These are not, of course, airtight compartments. The first group stresses the goal of the Good City, of community, of transforming drab impersonal surroundings into a warm, responsive, personally liberating environment allowing for the maximum flexibility and freedom for the individual. The second group sees the urban problem as the maintenance of the economic viability of the central city through increasing—or at least limiting the decrease of—real estate values, business earnings, and the resultant property taxes. Third are the demands of the urban poor, especially the blacks, which stress the need for better housing and schools, jobs, and adequate income supplements for those unable to work.

City officials therefore must consider three constituencies. While the first two groups exercise positive influence through political organizations and lobbyists of different sorts, the poor for the most part can exercise only a negative influence through violence and the threat of violence. There is an uneasy overlapping of interests between the needs of the middle-class urbanites who demand certain services from their cities on threat of leaving, and those responsible for the financial management of cities who need this higher-income group to finance the other needs of the city. Thus far, policy has been developed primarily to suit the needs of the latter two groups.

Concern with the financial needs of the city leads politicians to urban-renew city centers in order to raise property values. If in the process the poor get relocated, either to less valuable land within the city or into the next town, so much the better. Care of the poor takes resources which can be used elsewhere. Building the middle-class city, which involves attracting, holding, and helping businesses, cannot be pursued if the poor have first claim on the city's limited resources. But of course the poor do not have such a claim.

Urban problems and poverty are handled in an ad hoc and inefficient manner. Confusion about aims is matched by lack of commitment to genuine alleviation of these major social ills. Too many people gain from the status quo: owners of ghetto housing and small businesses, privileged white workers protected from black competition, employers who play upon each race's hatred against the other, and all who gain when society's dirty work is done cheaply by others.

A number of generalizations which can be made about black-white relations in the United States are of prime importance to understand if one wants to change the racist reality which prevails. First, substantial black deprivation, segregation, and exploitation do exist objectively. Second, these forms of discrimination are systematic, endemic to the form of internal colonialism that has been developed in this country. Third, they are continued because important segments of white society profit from such arrangements; therefore, while significant social legislation has been enacted, we find only token enforcement. Fourth, political influence follows economic power, and those with vested interests use their power to resist progressive reform. When change is allowed, either for appearance's sake or as the result of popular pressure, programs are set up in a manner which insures failure, or they are perverted to serve the interests of groups other than the poor. Fifth, a great number of structural reforms are needed (political and technological rationalization to organize production for use, not for profit; the termination of union restrictions against blacks, reflecting fear over job security and wage rates; the abolition of legal prohibitions, such as rigid and unreasonable building codes designed not for public safety but to create profit for the industry; abolition of large-lot zoning to keep the poor out, and so on). Such reforms are nearly impossible to bring about, because national priorities are, in the familiar terms, structured so as to preclude meaningful change.

These theses are typically debated on the most general level, a practice which is seldom convincing. Or the issues are avoided altogether by confining discussions exclusively to less value-laden and more narrowly defined problems. The remainder of this chapter will be devoted to the examination of a major area of concern—urban housing—where these generalizations will be shown to hold true.

By discussing one example in detail we cannot, of course, prove the general validity of these contentions, but we can suggest how government serves special interests and works in very important ways to allow and perpetuate the exploitation of blacks. As the example should make clear, such policies continue only because there exists a tacit (white) societal agreement that blacks as a group can be excluded. Housing is selected for special treatment because the physical separation of the ghetto is the most obvious aspect of black exploitation and segregation.

Housing and the Ghetto

America, viewed for a moment as a single entity, is in many ways a strange country. We are rich enough to abolish poverty, but too selfish to do so. We produce vast wealth, but live in the midst of squalor. Worse, we deny this reality. It is possible to point to the dramatic decline in substandard housing from 36.9 percent of the housing stock in 1950 to 19.5 percent a decade later, and an estimated 9.9 percent in 1970.[15] While the definition of *substandard* that is used can be criticized, such trends will usually be favorable with an increasing GNP. Certainly we are, as a nation, housed better than we were ten years ago. But this is to beg the question of present conditions. It is perhaps more important to understand the current situation and speak to its cause.

The literature on residential segregation is extensive and unanimous in concluding that there is a high degree of black segregation in metropolitan areas in all parts of the country, and that there has been a remarkable stability of this segregation pattern since the 1930s. Although earlier data are poor, this situation probably existed before that time as well.[16] While legal restrictions

[15] Frank S. Kristof, "Urban Needs and Economic Factors in Housing Policy," cited in Anthony Downs, "Moving toward Realistic Housing Goals," in *Agenda for the Nation*, ed. Kermit Gordon (Washington, D.C.: The Brookings Institution, 1968), p. 143.

[16] Karl E. Tauber and Alma F. Tauber, *Negroes in Cities* (Chicago: Aldine, 1965), especially pp. 78–95. See also David McIntire, *Residence and Race* (Berkeley, Calif.: University of California Press, 1960); and Chester Rapkin, "Price Discrimination against Negroes in the Rental Market," in *Essays in Urban Land Economics* (Los Angeles: Real Estate Research Program, University of California, 1966).

have been struck down by the courts, informal collusion, combined with harassment and violence, has maintained patterns of segregation.

The suggestion that low income excludes blacks from better neighborhoods is not borne out by the evidence on income and race. In 1960 only 12 percent of whites with incomes above the poverty level lived in poverty areas, while two-thirds of blacks who had incomes above the poverty level lived in poverty areas.[17] Numerous statistical studies have also concluded that socio-economic differences do not adequately explain urban racial residence patterns. A. H. Pascal reports, "That segregation of non-whites is widespread, intense, and of long duration in large American cities is the inescapable conclusion to be derived from the evidence presented. . . . [W]e can state that over 80 percent of the non-white population of Chicago and over 50 percent of the non-white population of Detroit would have to change its place of residence were segregation in these two metropolitan areas to be eliminated."[18]

Three conclusions emerge from these various studies. First, black-segregated residential patterns can be explained not by low income but by the working of "the exclusionary interests" ("real estate boards, suburban governments—that establish and maintain vast sanctuaries from Negroes and poor people").[19] Second, there is a great variety of available suburban housing. Studies show "a large supply of older low and moderate income housing already existing in many suburban communities. . . . *The existing suburban housing supply, in terms of housing cost, provides ample opportunity for desegregation now.*"[20] Third, government policies subsidize slumlords through lax or nonexistent code enforcement, thereby saving them millions of dollars; offer them generous tax treatment; and then pay them handsomely for their property when slums are bought under urban renewal. The economics of ghetto housing insures that bad housing is profitable and that good housing cannot

[17] U.S. Department of Health, Education and Welfare, *Toward a Social Report* (Washington, D.C.: Government Printing Office, 1969), p. 37.
[18] A. H. Pascal, *The Economics of Housing Segregation* (Santa Monica, Calif.: The Rand Corporation, 1967), p. 175.
[19] Alvin L. Schorr, *Explorations in Social Policy* (New York: Basic Books, 1968), p. 208.
[20] Richard Langendorf, "Residential Desegregation Potential," *Journal of the American Institute of Planners*, March 1969. Emphasis in original.

be maintained. There is a sort of Gresham's Law at work: bad housing drives out good; as neighborhoods deteriorate, further deterioration is induced.

This process continues because the owners of these buildings want to maximize their incomes. However, this fact does not indicate that slum housing in general is highly profitable. Given the unpleasantness and the risks involved, earnings may not be very good.[21] The point is rather that slum owners persist in their business because they make an adequate return, and that it is possible for the more disreputable and dishonest to do fairly well. Certainly the curtailment of existing practices through, for example, adequate code enforcement might bankrupt many marginally profitable operations. What profitably exists is the result of lack of law enforcement coupled with the existence of segregation.

The single most crucial factor in ensuring the profitability of slums is segregation. Timothy Cooney, a former city official in New York, gives a cynic's advice on "how to build a slum": "The importance of renting to minority families cannot be overemphasized . . . they are the key. . . . The all-white sections are essential to successful slum development. They must be maintained (until we decide to turn *them* into slums). The reason is obvious. With a 'whites only' barricade (or other slums) surrounding our developing slum, there will be no escape for our selected tenants."[22] Alvin Schorr describes the process in greater detail: "As buildings are subdivided, crowded, and more deteriorated, they become wellnigh impossible to maintain. However, it becomes impractical to try to maintain neighboring houses. They too become a profitable investment and slum development spirals. If the city steps in and tries to enforce codes strictly, some owners will be able to make no profit at all. They paid too high a price and counted on overcrowding. If it is suggested that the municipality take the houses over, paying for their reasonable value, it develops that this is less than the current owner paid for it. Why pick on him? Once begun, the cycle is not readily interrupted."[23] Change is made still more diffi-

---

[21] See George Sternlieb, *The Tenement Landlord* (New Brunswick, N.J.: Rutgers—The State University, Urban Studies Center, 1966).

[22] Timothy J. Cooney, "How to Build a Slum," *The Nation*, February 14, 1959, p. 141.

[23] Schorr, *Explorations in Social Policy*, p. 200.

cult because government policy encourages slum formation and perpetuation.

Housing and Government

On one level all that is required is an honest enforcement of the law. The burden of insuring that there are no code violations could even be placed on the property owner by having "the Internal Revenue Service disallow all depreciation allowances, property tax deductions, and interest deductions on properties in designated 'high deterioration' zones within large cities unless the owners' tax returns are accompanied by certificates of full code compliance issued by local authorities."[24] But would such a plan work? The answer is no. There are already laws against discrimination in renting and sale of apartments and houses. There are laws to ensure adequate plumbing and to enforce building codes, but the law is biased in favor of those who have some influence in the society. The blacks do not have such influence. Slum fires are so common that in some areas the sick joke goes around which asks if one has heard about the new instant urban renewal program; for the night before for the third (or fifth) time this month there has been a major fire in the ghetto. After one such fire in Brooklyn, New York, a grand jury investigated a fifteen-block area. It found 3,122 code violations; before the survey only 567 violations had been filed.[25] And of course little had been done about these 567. New York is not unique in its ratio of actual to reported violations. But because codes are often unclear, penalties slight, and enforcement staffs small, it is easier to ignore maintenance, not respond to warnings, and pay the small fine which eventually may be imposed, than to make repairs. "The hard fact is that profit-making incentives run counter—so far as the maintenance of housing is concerned—to the best interests of the poor. Tax laws and condemnation procedures combine with the peculiarly vulnerable situation of those who are poor to pay the most profit for the worst housing. Where enforcement is pitted day by day against the businessman's

---

[24] Anthony Downs, "Moving Toward Realistic Housing Goals," in *Agenda for the Nation*, ed. Kermit Gordon (Washington, D.C.: The Brookings Institution, 1968) p. 171.
[25] Schorr, *Explorations in Social Policy*, p. 200.

incentive to make profit, enforcement is bound to be in trouble."[26]

More than this, the whole system is predicated on the non-enforcement of the law. The code enforcement agencies could not possibly carry out their legal responsibility. If they did, landlords in large numbers would go bankrupt and tenants would be evicted as buildings were declared unfit for human habitation. Repair costs would in a great many instances prove more than the rental capacity of the building after repairs were made. "Just a modest step-up in enforcement activity under a new administration in New York City recently resulted in a rapid upsurge in the number of foreclosures, tax delinquencies, and vacate orders. When slumlords are pushed out, government has to house the minority poor. So the enforcement agencies use their powers gingerly and selectively, usually paying heed only when tenants have the tenacity or the 'pull' to compel enforcement. In other words, slum profits depend on collusion between city agencies and landlords: in return for non-enforcement of the codes, the slumlord takes the blame for the slum and enables the city to evade the political ire of the ghetto."[27]

The culpability of government, if that is the proper phrase, goes much deeper than not enforcing housing codes. Federal government policies into the 1960s consciously encouraged segregation. The Federal Housing Administration, which insures millions of dollars of mortgages, for many years took the position that racial homogeneity was essential to a neighborhood's financial stability. It therefore placed higher valuations on properties in neighborhoods that were white than in those that were mixed. This policy served as a powerful inducement to segregation. After restrictive racial covenants in deeds were held to be unconstitutional, the FHA stopped insuring properties where such covenants applied. But it continued to tolerate discrimination, providing insurance where builders would not sell, mortgagors would not lend, and owners would not rent to Negroes. In 1962, President Kennedy issued an executive order reversing this policy. The order forbade discrimination in the sale or rental of all housing owned or fin-

---

[26] *Ibid.*, p. 198.
[27] Francis Piven and Richard Cloward, "Disrupting City Services to Change National Priorities," *Viet-Report*, Summer 1968, p. 28.

anced by the government. But it applied only to future transactions; existing segregation was not disturbed.[28] At the same time that the FHA was encouraging segregation, it was redistributing real income from general taxation to the non-poor homeowners. Until August 1967, the FHA, by denying mortgage insurance programs to buyers in blighted areas (because such loan insurance was "economically unsound"), did not help blacks become homeowners in their own restricted housing markets. At the same time the white exodus was financed through FHA loans. As Michael Harrington has written, "It is one of the great postwar scandals that lavish, but discreet, subsidies have been provided for the homes of the middle class and the rich in the form of cheap, federally guaranteed credit, income tax deductions, and other genteel doles which effectively exclude everyone with incomes of less than $8,000 from the benefits."[29] The extent of this perverse redistribution can be only crudely estimated. One study presents the following data for 1962. The federal government spent $820 million to subsidize housing for the poor (this total includes public housing, public assistance, and tax deductions). That same year at least an estimated $2.9 billion was spent to subsidize housing for middle- and upper-income families.[30] This sum includes only savings from income-tax deductions and so is a very conservative estimate of housing subsidies to the non-poor. In his scheme to aid low-income people living in inadequate housing, Anthony Downs estimates that, assuming the federal government paid "only the marginal difference between the return demanded by the lenders and the amounts which households in inadequate units could afford to pay," subsidies amounting to $26 billion for the decade 1970–1980 (about the same amount spent on the space program in the decade 1960–1970) would be needed to do away with all substandard housing.[31] Such a plan would cost about the same amount as the subsidy that will be given to middle- and upper-income families in the same period.

[28] Clair Wilcox, *Toward Social Welfare* (Homewood, Ill.: Richard D. Irwin, 1969), p. 200.
[29] Michael Harrington, "Can Private Industry Abolish Slums?" *Dissent*, January-February 1968, p. 5.
[30] Schorr, *Explorations in Social Policy*, p. 208.
[31] Downs, "Moving toward Realistic Housing Goals," p. 161.

Federal Housing Policy

The artificially high demand for inferior ghetto housing results from segregation enforced through legal practices such as large-lot zoning which help keep lower-income (nonwhite) families out of suburbia, and illegal collusion, as when realtors refuse to sell to blacks. Ghetto housing is substandard because codes are not enforced and cannot be. The municipal property tax penalizes improvements and rewards poor maintenance. The use of earning power as a measure of determining value in condemnation procedures favors those who overcrowd their buildings. Capital-gains taxes and depreciation policies have improved somewhat but are still too generous to slum owners.

The two most important federal housing programs (after FHA insured loans) are public housing and urban renewal. Both have been hamstrung by regulations to insure that they cannot compete with, but can only complement, the workings of the private sector.

Public housing is built to be a badge identifying the poor. Projects are characterized by their ugliness and regimentation. In the minds of some, this is good. They are a warning against allowing the federal government to interfere. The same expenditure (about $25,000 a unit) could purchase a house in suburbia and a new car for the poor family, who then could live much like anybody else. Those who receive charity must carry the stigma of being public wards. In a class society part of one's evaluation of his own position as favorable stems from the distance between his income and standard of living and those of people who have less. This distance measures his success. Public housing must indicate the economic position of its residents.

Public housing has also failed in a quantitative sense, in that the number of units built has not begun to supply the demand of those qualifying for apartments. At the end of 1965 there were an estimated 600,000 units of public housing, with a waiting list of 500,000 families. There are about 8.5 million families who are eligible for public housing.[32] Because the waiting list is so long, many of those eligible do not bother to apply. At the same time

[32] Pascal, *The Economics of Housing Segregation*, p. 6.

public housing is not adding sufficiently to the housing stock, the supply of inexpensive housing is being diminished by urban renewal.

Urban renewal assembles large amounts of land and makes them available to private buyers at far less than they would have to pay on the open market. Poor families who reside in the renewal area are forced to relocate. Attempts are made to see that these families find standard housing at rents they can afford. However, if such housing were available, it is difficult to see why the people would have been living in slum housing. In any case, the supply of low-cost housing is diminished, pushing up rents, and making living more difficult for other low-income families looking for housing. The cleared land is then used to build middle- and upper-income housing or for industrial plants, or shopping centers.[33] In many cities urban renewal is called "Negro Removal," and many blacks see it as a land grab subsidized by the government and run by local real-estate interests.

There are federal housing policies which are designed to work in useful ways to help low-income people. One such program is rent supplements, under which the federal government pays the difference between what a family can afford to pay in rent (twenty-five percent of family income) and the rent a landlord can get on the free market. The family involved gets to live in adequate housing in a building with people of higher income and so is not stigmatized as "poor." The landlord receives adequate compensation, and the federal government's subsidy makes up the difference between what a family is able to pay and the cost of dwellings which meet minimum code standards. The program is obviously costly if subsidies go to very low-income families. Still, as incomes rise, subsidies diminish, and there is not the disincentive, as in public housing, where if a tenant's income rises beyond a certain point, he must move. Instead of government-run projects, rent subsidies leave housing rental to the private sector. However, the program is not

[33] See Jewel Bellush and Murray Hausknecht, ed., *Urban Renewal: People, Politics and Planning* (Garden City, N.Y.: Doubleday, 1967); James Q. Wilson, ed., *Urban Renewal: The Record and the Controversy* (Cambridge, Mass.: The M.I.T. Press, 1966); Charles Abrams, *The City Is the Frontier* (New York: Harper & Row, 1967); and Scott Greer, *Urban Renewal and American Cities* (Indianapolis: Bobbs-Merrill, 1965).

doing well in Congress, perhaps because taxpayers do not like to see "the poor get something for nothing," especially when that something is being able to live in conditions similar to those they have worked hard to provide for themselves. Dick Netzer has suggested some further reasons why this may be so: "Partly, this may be because of the extent of subsidy; in part, the explanation may be opposition to the degree of racial integration implicit in a program that provides for people with very different incomes living in the same building. At any rate, the program has been encumbered with many restrictions, and the funds authorized for it have been minimal. The number of new housing units actually built under the program has been very small indeed."[34]

We could be hopeful and say that since this program only started in 1965 maybe it will gain support and be funded at meaningful levels. If so it would be unique. The lack is not of economically sound ways of helping the urban poor, black and white. It is rather to be found in the societal attitude towards the poor, and especially minority-group poor.

To summarize what has been said about housing: blacks are excluded from equal participation in housing markets. They are exploited, forced by a racist society to pay for inferior housing. Discrimination is systematic and pervasive. It is perpetuated by those who profit from the existence of the ghetto, and by those who wish to maintain their privileged position in society. Enough legislation exists to end forced segregation, but it is consistently ignored. The present situation could not continue if this were not so. The federal housing programs which do exist often favor the rich and the middle class at the expense of the poor. Further, a few reforms cannot be really meaningful until new economic relations are established, until the private profit motivation for perpetuating slums is ended.

[34] Dick Netzer, *Economics and Urban Problems: Diagnoses and Prescriptions* (New York: Basic Books, 1970), p. 105.

CHAPTER 2

The Black Ghetto
as Colony

Urbanologists and students of poverty have written a great deal of descriptive material about the black ghetto. Studies have detailed the extent of poverty, the number of families headed by women, the prevalence of substandard housing, the inferior quality of public facilities, and so on. The sum of these bits and pieces has not, however, been incorporated into a very satisfactory analysis of the causes which have created the ghetto, or of the forces which perpetuate it.

Systematic discrimination sets off the vast majority of blacks from the rest of the working class. Since social status is measured by relative distance between identifiable groups, the existence of a black subclass forced to do the dirty work of the society allows whites to be better off—even as it creates fear that those below will move up.

The black ghetto is best viewed from the perspective of development economics. In its relations with the dominant white society, the black ghetto stands as a unit apart, an internal colony exploited in a systematic fashion. There are limits to such a parallel, but it is helpful as an organizational construct. Through it, current policy alternatives may be viewed in a more meaningful perspective than heretofore.

21

The Development Perspective

Introductory chapters of a standard development textbook present a description of the typical less-developed country: low per-capita income; high birth rate; a small, weak middle class; low rates of increase in labor productivity, capital formation, domestic savings; and a small monetized market.[1] The economy of such a country is heavily dependent on external markets where its few basic exports face an inelastic demand (that is, demand is relatively constant regardless of price, and so expanding total output may not mean higher earnings). The international demonstration effect (the desire to consume the products enjoyed in wealthier nations) works to increase the quantity of foreign goods imported, putting pressure on the balance of payments as the value of imports exceeds the value of exports. Much of the small modern sector of the economy is owned by outsiders. Local entrepreneurship is limited, and in the absence of intergovernmental transfers, things might be still worse for the residents of these areas.

The economic relations of the ghetto to white America closely parallel those between third-world nations and the industrially advanced countries. The ghetto also has a relatively low per-capita income and a high birth rate. Its residents are for the most part unskilled. Businesses lack capital and managerial know-how. Local markets are limited. The incidence of credit default is high. Little saving takes place and what is saved is usually not invested locally. Goods and services tend to be "imported" for the most part, only the simplest and the most labor-intensive being produced locally. The ghetto is dependent on one basic export—its unskilled labor power. Aggregate demand for this export does not increase to match the growth of the ghetto labor force, and unemployment is prevalent. As consumer goods are advertised twenty-four hours a day on radio and television, ghetto residents are constantly reminded of the availability of goods and services which they cannot afford to buy. Welfare payments and other governmental transfers are needed to help pay for the ghetto's requirements. Local busi-

[1] For example, see Everett E. Hagen, *The Economics of Development* (Homewood, Ill.: Richard D. Irwin, 1968), Part 1.

nesses are owned, in large numbers, by non-residents, many of whom are white. Important jobs in the local public economy (teachers, policemen, and postmen) are held by white outsiders. The black ghetto, then, is in many ways in a position similar to that of the typical underdeveloped nation. Can such relationships be termed colonial? And to what extent is the issue one of race and how much one of class?

Colonial Relationships

Until recent years any thought that discrimination against black people represented a colonial relationship was for the most part not accepted by white and black leadership. That segregation existed was acknowledged, that job discrimination was pervasive was clear, but that such a relationship was colonial was denied. In the post–civil rights era, some blacks, Malcolm X and Eldridge Cleaver, for example, looked at society not through the eyes of the well-educated, cultured, and relatively wealthy spokesmen of the NAACP or Urban League, but as outcasts from "respectable" society. From the outside, they looked at America, pronounced it racist, and declared that racism was part of the structure of the society. They likened the status of American blacks to that of the subjugated dark-skinned people around the world. They saw the relation of white to black in America as that of colonizers to colonized, oppressors to oppressed. Such militants saw white liberals who proclaimed themselves "color blind" and spoke of "equal rights for all" as hypocrites and worse. Love, understanding, and moral witness were not the weapons to use against one's exploiters. Just such "loyalty" allowed the British to dominate India for two centuries, or the French to control Algeria. Integration is possible only between equals. Since a colonial relation is inherently unequal, it must be broken before one can talk of integration.

There are two key relationships which must be proved to exist before the colonial analogy can be accepted: (1) economic control and exploitation, and (2) political dependence and subjugation. Both necessitate separation and inferior status. If these relationships can be demonstrated, the case can be made that, for meaningful long-run improvement to take place, the ghetto must break the shackles imposed by colonial exploitation.

In defining colonialism, militants argue that the spatial separation of colony and colonial power is secondary to the existence of control of the ghetto from the outside through political and economic domination by white society. An historical comparison of the forms colonialism has taken, and a description of the place of blacks in the American economy make clear that internal colonialism is an apt description of the place blacks have held and continue to hold in our society.

Internal Colonialism

The vast majority of colonies were established by Western powers over technologically less advanced peoples of Asia, Africa, and Latin America. Military supremacy, combined with judicious bribing of local leaders and a generous sprinkling of Christian missionaries, enabled an outside power to dominate an area spatially separate from the ruling state. In some colonies there was extensive settlement by Europeans. If the territory was relatively unpopulated (Canada, Australia, New Zealand, and the United States), a policy of genocide and of exchanging land for beads allowed the settlers to gain control. When their numbers and strength grew, the settlers could demand independence from the mother country. Nationhood was usually followed by continuing economic relationship, but on better terms than the colony had enjoyed before it became independent. In some of the cases where European settlement was large but still a small minority of the total population of the colony, often a long and bloody struggle for independence resulted.

The black experience in America was somewhat different. Here the colonized were brought to the "mother" country to be enslaved and exploited. Internal colonialism thus involved the conquest and subjugation of a people and their physical removal to the ruling state. The command of the resources of the captive people (their labor power) followed. To find parallel cases one must go back to the ancient history of Egypt, Greece, and Rome: in these nations slaves were also brought to the mother country to be exploited, to do the dirty work of these "great societies." The grandeur of the mother country was built on the backs of the exploited slaves.

In the United States an important part of the capital built up in the early nineteenth century also came from slave labor. Douglass North suggests that the timing and pace of an economy's development is determined by the success of its export sector and the disposition of the income received by the export sector.[2] He argues that in the key years in which capital accumulation took place, "it was the growth of the cotton textile industry and the demand for cotton which was decisive."[3] The "vicissitudes of the cotton trade were the most important influence upon the varying rates of growth in the economy during the period."[4] That New England merchants, through their control over the foreign trade and commerce of the country, and over insurance and shipping, did much of the actual accumulating should not be allowed to obscure this point. Cotton was the strategic variable. It paid for our imports, and "the demand for western foodstuffs and northeastern services and manufactures was basically dependent upon the income received from the cotton trade."[5] This is not an attempt to single out one factor as providing the "key" to development. But cotton was the "carrier" industry inducing economic growth, and slavery was the basis of cotton production. Often the terrible burden of slavery is acknowledged, but rarely is the contribution of slave labor to the capital accumulation process seen as the very sizable factor in American development that it truly was.

In the post-Civil War period the place of blacks in the economy becomes more ambiguous, but in terms of understanding the present situation, the period is most significant. It is in this period that racial strife becomes built into the social fabric, making joint action by poor whites and blacks extremely difficult. The "free" blacks served the function of an equilibrating factor in the economy. They could hold jobs nobody else wanted, do the dirty work of the so-

---

[2] Douglass C. North, *The Economic Growth of the United States, 1790–1860* (Englewood Cliffs, N.J.: Prentice-Hall, 1961), p. 67; also a Norton Library paperback, 1966.
[3] *Ibid.*
[4] *Ibid.*
[5] *Ibid.*

ciety, and be called upon for higher-paying jobs in periods of labor shortage. In slack periods, blacks could be fired to make room for unemployed whites. Blacks were used as strikebreakers in coal and iron mines, steel mills, lumber camps, meat packing plants, and other industries.[6]

The jobs that blacks were recruited for in the labor shortages of World War I and the prosperity of the 1920s were taken away in the Depression. Arthur Ross has written:

> There was widespread invasion of Negro jobs by unemployed whites, often with the assistance of employers, unions, and lawmakers. Municipal licensing ordinances were reviewed in the South in order to drive Negroes out of barbering, plumbing, and other new occupations Negroes had entered during recent years.[7]

While the Depression hit blacks particularly hard because of the disastrous drop in agricultural earnings (especially in cotton) and the loss of urban jobs to whites, "Negroes frequently were able to earn more on work relief than they could have obtained in private employment if jobs had been available."[8]

World War II brought job opportunities for blacks, as did the Korean and Vietnam wars, but the quality of the jobs and the wages typically paid blacks corresponded to their low status in the economy.

Precise prediction of labor-force needs in the decades to come is an uncertain undertaking, but the informed consensus stresses the continued declining need for unskilled labor and an increasing premium on an educated labor force. If this is so, an unskilled, uneducated black population may make relatively less of a contribution. The needs of the society have changed. Still, blacks remain in their historic position somewhere between Marx's reserve army and Cairnes's non-competing group. That is, they are an available source of labor when needed by the economy and at the same time a group set apart which can be confined to certain types of work

---

[6] Arthur M. Ross, "The Negro in the American Economy," in *Employment, Race, and Poverty*, ed. Arthur M. Ross and Herbert Hill (New York: Harcourt, Brace & World, 1967), p. 12.
[7] *Ibid.*, p. 15.
[8] *Ibid.*, p. 16.

(low-paying, hard, and unpleasant jobs). They have been given the worst jobs the society had to offer. When labor is scarce they are given the lower rungs of better jobs; when economic conditions decline, whites move in to take even the jobs previously set aside as "Negro work." The blacks act as a buffer pool, keeping labor costs from rising. In this way the entire white society benefits by receiving goods and services more cheaply and white unemployment is cushioned.

Maintaining the Colony

In any colony there is always room for bright natives to hold responsible and important positions—though not at the very top. Education and the acceptance of the goals and outlook of the colonial power were (and are) the requisites for the acquisition of such jobs by natives. These acculturated natives can serve as minor functionaries in the ghetto, as they did extensively in the British empire. They can act as middlemen between other natives and the colonist businessmen who can then reside "abroad." Natives who are brought into the system not only directly serve the colonial power but also are examples to others of how working hard within the system can bring advancement. Their success suggests that others who work can make it as well, and that those who do not are to blame for their own failure. Analogous positions have always been available for limited numbers of American blacks. However, the vast majority are excluded from higher-status positions through a network of economic, social, and political barriers. How these barriers function is easily understood in the colonial context. Consider the place of educational barriers to black advancement.

In a technological and information-oriented economy, education is an increasingly crucial resource. The importance of human capital in American development has been adequately demonstrated in recent years.[9] One commentator has gone so far as to suggest that Europe is in danger of becoming an economic colony of the United

[9] See M. Abramovitz, "Economic Growth in the United States," *American Economic Review*, September 1962; and E. F. Denison, "Measuring the Contribution of Education (and the Residual) to Economic Growth," in *The Residual Factor and Economic Growth* (Paris: Organization for Economic Cooperation and Development, 1964).

States because of our more advanced technological and organizational abilities.[10] In such an economy, as a recent HEW report suggests, "one way in which high status parents can assure the future success of their children is by providing them with a better than average education."[11] The striking difference in quality among our schools is evidence that some groups do in fact get better education than others. More interesting is the finding that even for high school graduates with the same high academic aptitudes (the top one-fifth), if the parents are in the top socio-economic quartile, then 82 percent go to college in the first year after high school graduation, but if parents are from the bottom socio-economic quartile, only 37 percent go to college in the first year after graduation. Higher-income children with much lower ability are more likely to go to college than poor children with top ability. The chances of graduate school are even more remote for talented children from lower socio-economic groups.[12] These findings may be combined with the class bias of I.Q. and other "objective" tests of ability to demonstrate that our schools do to a large degree perpetuate class and racial barriers.

While higher socio-economic status is of great importance in predicting white educational advancement, it is a poor predictor for blacks. The HEW report analyzes the problem as follows:

> Most Negro men, *regardless of their fathers' occupations*, were working at unskilled or semiskilled jobs. Even if their fathers were in professional, managerial, or proprietary positions, they were usually operatives, service workers, or laborers. Growing up in a family of high socio-economic status was only a slight advantage for the Negro man. By contrast, the majority of white men with higher white collar backgrounds remained at their fathers' level and almost half of the white men whose fathers were in clerical or sales work and almost two-fifths of those with a farm or blue collar background moved up into the more prestigious professional and managerial group. But the Negroes from similar origins did not. The Negro man originating at the lower levels is likely to stay there, the

[10] Jean-Jacques Servan-Schreiber, *The American Challenge* (New York: Atheneum, 1968).
[11] U.S. Department of Health, Education and Welfare, *Toward a Social Report* (Washington, D.C.: Government Printing Office, 1969), p. 20.
[12] *Ibid.*

white man to move up. The Negro originating at the higher levels is likely to move down; the white man seldom does. The contrast is stark.[13]

A recent study, sponsored by the Southern Education Reporting Service and the National Association of State Universities and Land Grant Colleges, and conducted by John Egerton, concludes that "desegregation in state universities has been talked about, declared, implied and assumed to be substantial for years" but "has in fact, been largely token." (Less than two percent of the students in 1968 at major state universities were black.[14]) Thus even before black youths enter the labor force, their job prospects, assuming the absence of labor union and employer discrimination, are poor. The black worker's place in the economy is similar to that of the native's in the colony. He owns little and must work at the lowest-paying jobs. The majority of blacks seek work in a restricted labor market. As Michael Piore has written:

> The manpower problems of the urban ghetto appear best defined in terms of a dual labor market: a *primary* market offering relatively high-paying, stable employment, with good working conditions, chances of advancement and equitable administration of work rules; and a *secondary* market, to which the urban poor are confined, decidedly less attractive in all of these respects and in direct competition with welfare and crime for the attachment of the potential labor force.[15]

The complaints of white employers about their black employees also offer interesting parallels to the comments made by foreign businessmen in the colonies. The workers, it is charged, "show up late to work. They lack discipline, learn slowly, and don't stay on the job very long. They are not as good as white workers." All of these characteristics are real enough, but they are conditioned by the work-force experience of blacks and are reinforced within the context of secondary labor markets. There is not much reason to

---

[13] *Ibid.*, pp. 23–24.
[14] *The New York Times*, June 18, 1969, p. 1.
[15] Michael J. Piore, "Public and Private Responsibility in On-the-Job Training of Disadvantaged Workers," *Department of Economics Working Paper*, Number 23 (Cambridge, Mass.: The M.I.T. Press, June 1968), pp. 2–3.

work hard when the reward for such effort is not advancement, but merely the establishment of a higher work norm.

Strong comparisons are also possible in political terms between the ghetto and the third-world colony. When we ask the question, "Who controls the institutions of power?" the answer is the same in both cases—outsiders. The ghetto feels itself oppressed by a foreign army of occupation—the police—and is generally unable to determine how things will be done in its own community. The ghetto elects political leaders, but these men are caught in much the same frustrating bind as the elected leaders of newly independent nations. They are dependent on political and economic power outside the ghetto if they are to achieve anything for their people. "Foreign aid," whether to a new nation or to the ghetto, comes at a price of cooperation and compromise. Such an imbalance of political power is often hard to distinguish from neo-colonialism.

While ethnic accommodation has been a familiar historic pattern in American politics, with very few exceptions, blacks have not been organized as a powerful voting bloc under black leadership to gain political favors in proportion to their voting strength. Nor have blacks until fairly recently been concentrated in urban areas in large enough numbers to outvote whites who have not been willing, in any great number, to vote for black candidates. This has been true regardless of the candidates' and indeed the voters' politics.

The Choices

In many ways the options open to the black ghetto are similar to those of the developing nation. For each the crucial question is how much foreign influence is desirable. A nation may invite foreign capital in, allow for complete foreign control of its key sectors, and permit repatriation of profit and principal at the will of the investors. At the other extreme, a country can forgo foreign capital, management, and markets and opt for complete autonomy. The latter course means a break with past social, political, and economic institutions. It calls for the total mobilization of the energies and resources of the country to substitute for resources which formerly were available from abroad. This has proven a difficult challenge when attempted by nations like Cuba and China. It is questionable whether regions which are part of a nation can successfully develop independent of external controls. The analogy therefore reaches its limit at this point.

While riots can be seen in terms of " 'expropriating the expropriators,' "[16] the black community can gain only a limited independence. Blacks in the final analysis are Americans. They do not live in a territory which could become independent. Given their own nation by rearranging white and blacks in an India-Paskistan type of division makes little sense. The blacks would still be poor and still be limited to a dependent status which would be no more than a neo-colonialism in which they exported labor-intensive products and imported most sophisticated goods from the dominant white nation. Blacks must either be integrated into the society or establish a tenuous independence within the white nation. How great the ghetto's autonomy would be would depend on the collective identity of blacks as blacks and their willingness to press demands and obtain political power. However, there are narrow limits to what determined blacks can do, even when they win political control of a whole city. Richard Hatcher, the mayor of Gary, Indiana, commented in a speech that his electoral success had not brought about meaningful black control: "There is much talk about black control of the ghetto," he said. "What does that mean? I am mayor of a city of roughly 90,000 black people, but we do not control the possibilities of jobs for them, of money for their schools, or state-funded social services. These things are in the hands of the United States Steel Corporation and the County Department of Welfare of the State of Indiana. Will the poor in Gary's worst slums be helped because the pawn-shop owner is black, not white?"[17]

Black people could run the schools, the libraries, and the local parks, but to get money they would have to go outside the ghetto. Once black leaders are chosen and start dealing with those who

[16] See Robert Blauner, "Internal Colonialism and Ghetto Revolt," *Social Problems,* Spring 1969.
[17] Cited by Robert L. Allen, *Black Awakening in Capitalist America: An Analytic History* (Garden City, N.Y.: Doubleday, 1969), p. 117*n.*

hold real power, they will find that in order to get concessions they must first get rid of the militants who are "causing trouble and alienating the whites." This type of political pressure will probably be combined with efforts to create a middle class among blacks: homeowners and black capitalists. Such a group would serve as a bulwark against "those who would tear at the fabric of our society." The argument is often presented: "Give these people a piece of the action, a stake in America." In addition to the carrot of ownership for an enlarged middle class, manpower training for a growing working class, and welfare for the rest, there is still the tactical police force and other counterinsurgency forces.

There are, therefore, strong pressures to work within the system. Arthur Lewis, a prominent black economist, has urged black students to stop pushing for separate black programs and work instead to get more rigorous training as chemists, engineers, and economists. The neighborhood, he believes, is not the important focal point for action. Lewis suggests that black success is measured by how many blacks "become top members of the establishment."[18] Lewis stresses the limits of a movement for neighborhood autonomy. "There will be black grocery shops in black neighborhoods, but in your lifetime and mine," Lewis wrote, "there isn't going to be a black General Motors, a black Union Carbide. . . ."[19] Lewis ignores the reasons blacks attack a free enterprise system which has "chosen" to hire blacks last and fire them first. Entry into better jobs for individual blacks has come only recently, as a result of pressure by black mass action.

The possibilities for change open to a purely black social movement are limited by the minority position of blacks in a white society. For this reason Lewis counsels blacks to obtain better education so they can compete for jobs at General Motors. Through involvement in such powerful economic institutions, blacks can advance their cause. While Lewis does not accept the colonial analogy, the advice he offers ghetto residents is similar to that often given to newly independent nations—invite foreign business in by giving them advantageous terms, and foster cooperation with these

[18] W. Arthur Lewis, "The Road to the Top Is through Higher Education—Not Black Studies," *The New York Times Magazine,* May 11, 1969.
[19] *Ibid.,* p. 40.

firms so that local entrepreneurship will develop. Critics of this approach term it neo-colonialism. They say that foreign firms will exploit the local economy.

In this country the very large firms project an image of concern. They initiate training programs for ghetto workers. Their presidents serve as chairmen of local Urban Coalition groups. At the same time, black militants are suspicious of these firms. Corporation executives have great political power. They are listened to in the councils of government. Militants ask, "How could the ghetto remain a colony if these men did not permit this to be so?" Like Eldridge Cleaver, for example, they see General Motors not as a bastion of strength which may be entered, but as one which must be destroyed. Cleaver believes corporations know that black strength is not in their interest. "White General Motors . . . knows that the unity of these twenty million ragamuffins will spell the death of the system. . . . At all costs, then, they will seek to keep these blacks from uniting, from becoming bold and revolutionary. These white property owners know that they must keep the blacks cowardly and intimidated."[20]

The dismantling of the colonial barriers against blacks carries with it a challenge to the corporate sector, an implicit threat to the dominant position of the profit motive as the determining factor in guiding production decisions. The black colony is forced to demand just such changes. If the wealth of America is to be shared on a more "equitable" basis, new rationales for distribution will have to be developed. Unlike overseas colonies which can win their freedom and go their own way, blacks must remake the total economic and social system in America if they wish to change their own situation.

An equally important obstacle to black liberation is the working-class white who is not too far ahead of the average black. Members of the white working class find that their tax burden has been rising. They resist income transfers to those below them, for they would have to pay for them. Their relative status is also diminished if blacks rise in social and economic position. The working-class white is apt to feel a general discontent, and his cultural

[20] Eldridge Cleaver, *Soul on Ice* (New York: McGraw-Hill, 1968), pp. 136–137.

background and educational training lead him to accept demonological interpretations for the sources of the evils which afflict him. He is hostile to ideas he views as foreign and often has very strong racial prejudices.[21] He sees his enemy as the blacks who want to take his job and the welfare mother who wants something for nothing, while he pays for her illegitimate children out of his ever-rising taxes. He does not see his enemy as the corporate elite which has sold him on consumerism and taught him to decry "big government" and "wasteful spending." It would seem that the white worker, tired from long hours of essentially meaningless work, wants to escape through the possession of more private goods. When black demands threaten what he has built up for himself and his family, he is unlikely to respond with understanding and generosity. While it is important to realize the extent of hostility among white workers, the growth of counter trends should not be ignored. Many white workers reject racism, both on a personal level and as harmful to their long-term class interests.

It seems likely that white society in the 1970s will continue to accept limited numbers of gifted blacks who work their way up. More than this will not come very easily. "Given a choice between a massive freedom budget and a police state, the American electorate is more likely to choose the latter."[22]

The type of policies which will probably get government endorsement in the coming years is likely to be neither a massive reallocation of national resources to serve the needs of our low-income groups, nor the acceptance of a police state. Before the latter is forced on the nation there are a number of reforms which can be attempted. Some of these are discussed in the next two chapters.

---

[21] See Seymour Martin Lipset, "Working-class Authoritarianism," in *Political Man: The Social Basis of Politics* (Garden City, N.Y.: Doubleday, 1960).
[22] Lewis M. Killian, *The Impossible Revolution* (New York: Random House, 1968), p. 173.

CHAPTER 3

Black Power —
Green Power

If the ghetto is viewed as an internal colony, it becomes easier to see why white political and corporate leaders are working so hard to convince ghetto dwellers that what they really want is "black capitalism." However, the idea of black capitalism runs counter to an important anti-capitalist strand in the black power ideology.[1]

Black power demands black control over black institutions. This can be achieved in two ways. Individual blacks may own the important resources of the ghetto, or the black community may, in common, own and run its economy. Increasingly blacks are choosing the second course. The "white power structure," on the other hand, prefers individual ownership by blacks, which of necessity will have to be in cooperation with outside white interests. The reason for this choice is apparent. Such an arrangement is amenable to neo-colonial rule, since it guarantees the indirect control of the ghetto economy through a local native class essentially dependent on larger white businesses. The aim is twofold: to win

---

[1] See Raymond S. Franklin, "The Political Economy of Black Power," *Social Problems*, Winter 1969; and Robert Blauner, "Internal Colonialism and Ghetto Revolt," *Social Problems*, Spring 1969.

loyalty of an important group of potentially influential local leaders, and to channel protest into less threatening, and incidentally, less useful goals. In this light, increasing the number of ghetto blacks in ownership positions appears to be an important prerequisite for ending ghetto unrest.[2] If blacks are upset because they lack control over the institutions of the ghetto, because they are charged high prices for inferior merchandise, victimized by credit racketeers, and exploited by employers, then perhaps—some would argue—greater black ownership will help end these conditions (or at least lessen anti-white feelings because the local merchants would be black). If the ghetto lacks leadership and a stable middle class, then enlarging the number of black entrepreneurs may provide such leadership and foster stability. If the problem is lack of racial confidence, the success of black capitalists would build pride. If riots are caused by people who have tenuous allegiance to our system, ownership is the best way to build a commitment to working for change within the system. Increasing the ownership class, in short, is a way to add stability, increase local leadership, lessen the visibility of white domination of the ghetto economy, and funnel ghetto discontent into acceptable channels.

Interest in black capitalism also strikes a responsive chord in the corporate sector. Proposals for black capitalism involve minimal direct government intervention. They provide for subsidies to cooperating private firms. Even though black hostility toward white businesses is increasing, the "Negro market, a market expected to reach $52 billion in 1975,"[3] cannot be ignored by even the largest firms. Market penetration is possible through joint corporations partly owned or managed by blacks. Franchising local blacks to distribute products in the ghetto and setting up independently owned but captive suppliers may also be in the corporation's interest. Banks limited by law to city boundaries find that as the black population grows they need to make more loans to minority-group businessmen to maintain their profit position.[4] Labor shortages in a period of rapid growth have sent many firms out to

[2] See, for example, Robert B. McKersie, "Vitalize Black Enterprise," *Harvard Business Review*, September–October 1968.
[3] "The Soul Market in Black and White," *Sales Management: The Marketing Magazine*, June 1, 1969.
[4] See *Christian Science Monitor*, July 9, 1968.

recruit in the ghetto, spurred on by Manpower Development and Training Act (MDTA) funds and a desire to get on better with the increasingly large number of blacks living in the inner city where their plants are located. Thus pushed by the demands of the black community and pulled by societal and corporate interest, government, industry, and black organizations are moving to promote black capitalism.

The purpose of this chapter is to assess the likely success of such efforts and to evaluate the strength and the nature of resistance to black capitalism. Three variations on the theme will be considered: attempts to help individual black small businesses, white corporate involvement in the ghetto, and proposals for community development corporations. Finally, different patterns of ghetto development and their impact on the economic structure of the ghetto will be considered. But it is first necessary to describe the ghetto marketplace itself.

The Ghetto Merchant and the Consumer

Some economists draw a contrast between how markets work in the ghetto and how they operate elsewhere. There are differences, to be sure, but they should not be allowed to obscure the essential fact that the market mechanism works in the ghetto pretty much in the way traditional theory would lead us to expect. Low-income people, lacking purchasing power and information concerning the quality of available merchandise, and restricted to shopping in ghetto markets, end up with inferior merchandise at higher prices. Seeking to maximize profit, the ghetto merchants adjust their sales practices to the nature of their customers, who are characterized as having low incomes and comparatively limited education.

Shady business practices are often reported in ghetto areas: use of bait advertising of goods which are "sold out" when the customer arrives; the switch sale, where the customer comes in to look at specials and is told that the special is not of good quality and what he really wants is some more expensive item; the refusal to return deposits; the misrepresentative sales contract; the used furniture sold as new; the coercive pressures on buyers; the attempts to collect non-existent debts. All these practices so frequently complained of have their roots in the powerlessness and the lack of educational and financial resources of the urban poor. Deliberation in buying durable goods, surveys find, is more highly correlated with education than with income.[5] Judging quality in consumer durables takes some skill, and understanding credit arrangements is not easy. With a low income, one naturally is on the lookout for a "good deal."

A specialized sales network has developed to deal with low-income people. The friendly smooth-talking dealer who makes the uneducated, poorly-dressed customer feel at home, gaining his confidence, offering generous credit terms impossible to obtain elsewhere—and all this right in his own neighborhood—is much easier to deal with than a hostile downtown department store salesman. However, the prices paid reflect this special service. A recent Federal Trade Commission (FTC) report concludes:

> The low-income market is a very expensive place to buy durable goods. On television sets (most of which are the popular 19-inch black and white portables), the general market retailer price is about $130. In the low-income market a customer can pay up to $250 for similar sets. Other comparisons include a dryer selling for $149.95 from a general market retailer and for $299.95 from a low-income market retailer; and a vacuum cleaner selling for $59.95 in the general market and $79.95 in the low-income market.[6]

The same FTC study found investment credit used more extensively by retailers selling in low-income neighborhoods than by retailers selling to consumers elsewhere.[7] Further, given the greater risks involved, much higher carrying charges are exacted in ghetto stores than on the general market.

Speaking of the reluctance of the poor to seek legal aid even when they have clearly been victimized, Mary Gardiner Jones, an

[5] See Louise G. Richards, "Consumer Practices of the Poor," in *The Ghetto as Marketplace*, ed. Frank D. Sturdivant (New York: The Free Press, 1969), p. 51.
[6] Federal Trade Commission, "Economic Report on Installment Credit and Retail Sales Practices of District of Columbia Retailers," in Sturdivant, *The Ghetto as Marketplace*, p. 101.
[7] *Ibid.*, p. 77.

FTC commissioner, says the problem is not only that the poor lack financial resources to get legal assistance:

> With the poor, this reluctance is aggravated by their unfortunately realistic fears of retaliation by the merchant or credit agency on whom they are so dependent, by their inabilities to express themselves in the language of the Establishment and by their sense of inferiority, hopelessness and general mistrust of any government authority, which they regard not as the protector of their rights, but as the body which puts them into jail, evicts them from their apartment or garnishes their salary.[8]

This sort of explanation is not sufficient. The legal system does favor the businessman over the ghetto resident. Garnishing of salaries for nonpayment of debt is relatively easy, even when the debts were contracted in ignorance and the contract obtained by fraud. The small print on installment contracts, unread by the buyer, allows for easy repossession. The city marshals, paid by the taxpayer to act as collection agents, earn a commission for their services. The entire legal system is set up to protect property and ensure contracts. Nor is the Better Business Bureau of much help to the low-income consumer. Not only has it no legal enforcement power, but it serves as a lightning rod, absorbing anger while protecting both the image and the profits of business.

> Its claims notwithstanding, the Better Business Bureau is little more than a businessman's protective association often syphoning off consumer complaints that would be better directed to other agencies. That it has less than the consumer's interest at heart is indicated by the fact that in many states it has lobbied against consumer representation in government on the false premise that the Bureau is already doing the job of protecting the customers.[9]

David Caplovitz, whose studies of consumer practices of low-income families brought the unscrupulous dealings of ghetto mer-

[8] Mary Gardiner Jones, "Deception in the Marketplace of the Poor: The Role of the Federal Trade Commission," in Sturdivant, *The Ghetto as Marketplace*, p. 252.
[9] David Caplovitz, *The Poor Pay More: Consumer Practices of Low Income Families* (New York: The Free Press, 1967), p. xxiii.

chants to the attention of the general public, has suggested that he may have "unwittingly created the impression ... that these problems exist only because of a small class of disreputable sellers."[10] Caplovitz points out that the sellers could not exist without the banks and finance companies which buy up dishonestly obtained contracts. The finance companies know what they are doing, as do the highly respected banks who lend to the finance companies.[11] The involvement of the financial community in the exploitation of the poor is similar here to the role it plays in perpetuating housing segregation.

Again, as in the case of the slum landlord, the typical ghetto merchant does not appear to be making high profits. The market, with a large number of buyers and sellers and ease of entry and exit, assures that only normal profits are earned in the long run. In addition, the major studies in this area all show that marketing goods to low-income consumers is costly. Insurance premiums are high, pilfering and robbery are major problems, and the use of salesmen who canvass on a house-to-house basis, make home demonstrations, and collect debts are expensive. Summarizing a study of durable goods merchants, the FTC reports: "Practically all of the substantially higher gross margin of the low-income market retailers were offset by higher expenses and did not result in markedly higher net profits as a percentage of sales."[12]

It seems doubtful that exchanging black merchants for white in ghetto stores would make much of a difference, given the realities of doing business in the ghetto. The discussion of black capitalism which follows must be seen in the light of these economic realities.

Black Capitalists

The small size of the black business class has generally been explained in two ways. First, there are barriers to an individual's advancement in business because he is black. Second, the nature of segregation and the economic relations between the black ghetto

[10] *Ibid.*, p. xvii.
[11] *Ibid.*, p. xvi.
[12] Federal Trade Commission, "Economic Report on Installment Credit," p. 104.

and the white society preclude, for the most part, the possibility of successful black businesses. Stressing one of these approaches over the other has major policy consequences; if blacks have not been successful because of discrimination, then classic civil rights strategies of groups like the Urban League and the NAACP should be followed. If the ghetto is viewed as an internal colony requiring collective liberation, then other strategies are called for.

Many scholars have pointed out the conspicuous absence of blacks in managerial and proprietary positions.[13] It has been argued that this situation exists because blacks are arriving in the cities at a time when opportunities for the establishment of small businesses are on the decline.[14] This may well be true, but the black man's failure to achieve success as a businessman must certainly be attributed more centrally to racism. As Eugene Foley has written, "The culture has simultaneously unduly emphasized achievement in business as the primary symbol of success and has blindly developed or imposed an all-pervading racism that denied the Negro the necessary opportunities for achieving this success."[15]

The only area in which black businessmen were able to gain entry was within their own segregated communities. In this regard the closing off of the ghetto may have helped black businessmen as a group. But even in the ghetto other groups often have the most prosperous businesses. In many cities Jews are more heavily represented in retail businesses than other groups as a result of past European restrictions on Jews which forced a disproportionate number to become traders and merchants because other professions were closed to them. Of the immigrant groups to come to America the Jews were as a result the group whose members went heavily into trade. In many ghettos anti-white feeling against merchants has taken on strong anti-semitic tones. However, a study of New Orleans, where the black ghetto businesses are heavily owned

---

[13] See, for example, Nathan Glazer and Daniel Patrick Moynihan, *Beyond the Melting Pot* (Cambridge, Mass.: The M.I.T. Press and Harvard University Press, 1963), pp. 31–32; and Daniel Patrick Moynihan, "Employment, Income, and the Ordeal of the Negro Family," in *The Negro American*, ed. Talcott Parsons and Kenneth B. Clark (Boston: Beacon Press, 1967), p. 143.
[14] Glazer and Moynihan, *Beyond the Melting Pot*, p. 143.
[15] Eugene P. Foley, "The Negro Businessman: In Search of a Tradition," in Parsons and Clark, *The Negro American*, p. 572.

by Italians, showed the presence of strong anti-Italian feeling. In all cases hatred is aimed at the group which economically dominates the ghetto.[16]

In getting started in business the European immigrants had three major advantages over the blacks. First, the immigrants usually had a sense of clannishness. Glazer and Moynihan point out that because of such group solidarity, funds were more readily available. "Those who had advanced themselves created little pools for ethnic businessmen and professionals to tap."[17] This has not been as true of blacks, until the present decade, when a sense of identity and group pride has developed among a sizable number of blacks. Second, there is the legacy of slavery. Blacks have not only the "badge of color but also the ingrained burden of generations of cultural and economic deprivation."[18]

> The plantation system offered the Negro no experience with money, no incentive to save, no conception of time or progress— none of the basic experience to prepare him for the urban money economy. Instead, it indoctrinated him to believe in his own inferiority, to be resigned, while it held him in a folk culture dominated by a spiritual, other-worldly, escapist outlook. . . .[19]

This is a limited view of the effects of slavery. It ignores the "calculated cruelty . . . designed to crush the spirit," the malice and the hatred which blacks endured under slavery. Nor does such a view speak to the continuing record.

"When slavery ended and large scale physical abuse was discontinued, it was supplanted by different but equally damaging abuse. The cruelty continued unabated in thoughts, feelings, intimidation and occasional lynching. Black people were consigned to a place outside the human family and the whip of the plantation was replaced by the boundaries of the ghetto."[20]

[16] St. Clair Drake and Horace R. Clayton, *Black Metropolis*, vol. II (second edition; New York: Harcourt, Brace and World, 1962), p. 432.
[17] Glazer and Moynihan, *Beyond the Melting Pot*, p. 33.
[18] Jeanne R. Lowe, *Cities in a Race with Time* (New York: Vintage, 1967), p. 283.
[19] *Ibid.*, p. 283.
[20] Grier and Cobbs, *Black Rage*, p. 20.

Whether one blames the dominance of folk culture or at a more fundamental level the limits slavery placed on black development, it may be concluded that blacks do lack "managerial skills and attitudes. Negroes as a race have been little exposed to business operations and lack technical experience and entrepreneurial values that are necessary for succeeding in business."[21]

In the 1920s and 1930s West Indian-born blacks coming to this country did very well as a group, going into business and proving quite successful. They had drive and determination to succeed, and did so in surprisingly large numbers. Sociologists have attributed their success to the Jamaican social structure, where in spite of British colonial administration rule, there was upward mobility for blacks. Coming to this country, West Indians had separate customs and accents and an identity distinct from the masses of black descendants of American slaves. The Jamaicans showed the same self-confidence and motivation as did other immigrant groups.[22] While this experience is not conclusive evidence, certainly enough has been written about the debilitating effect of the slavery experience that it must be counted high as a cause of the lack of black entrepreneurship. It is also of interest to note that the race pride and self-help ethic preached by the Black Muslims may well be responsible for their success in numerous ghetto-based business operations.

A third and last factor, also difficult to assess, is the importance of an economic base in some occupation or trade in which the group has a special advantage—a phenomenon not found among the black population.

Thus the Chinese in America, a small group who never dreamed until World War II of getting jobs in the general American community, had an economic base in laundries and restaurants—a peculiar base, but one that gave economic security and the wherewithal to send children to college. It has been estimated that the income of Chinese from Chinese-owned business is, in proportion to their numbers, *forty-five* times as great as the income of Negroes from Negro-owned business.[23]

[21] McKersie, "Vitalize Black Enterprise," p. 90.
[22] Glazer and Moynihan, *Beyond the Melting Pot*, p. 34.
[23] *Ibid.*, p. 37.

The lack of a business tradition may in and of itself be a handicap of some significance. The businessman is an important customer for other businessmen, and Italian bakeries are more likely to hire Italian truckers, suppliers, and so on.[24] Such ties are both natural and important. This is why black groups use their buying power to force white-owned businesses to hire black sales personnel. Black ownership could lead to the informal formation of "black" forward and backward linkages in procurement and sales patterns.

Another disadvantage the black businessman has is that he is limited to the ghetto as a place of business. This means that his customers have lower incomes than those of businessmen located elsewhere; his insurance rates, if indeed he can get insurance at all, tend to be much higher than elsewhere;[25] his customers are worse credit risks; loss rates from theft are higher; and so on. Further, when the black businessman goes to get bank loans, all of these disadvantages are thrown back at him. A commercial loan is "based on the proven management ability of the borrower in a stable industry and a stable locality."[26] Black businesses are for the most part marginal, unstable, and very poor credit risks. They also tend to be almost exclusively in retail and service trades. If "there exists, among Negroes, a rather low image of the significance and possibilities of business endeavors,"[27] this feeling seems justified. The evidence available suggests a low rate of return for black entrepreneurs.

There are black businessmen who have grown quite wealthy and others who are modestly well-to-do who have built up sizable businesses in the black communities of Atlanta, Durham, Chicago, and New York, but they have done so by overcoming extensive

[24] *Ibid.*, p. 31.
[25] See The President's National Advisory Panel on Insurance in Riot-Affected Areas, *Meeting the Insurance Crisis of Our Cities* (Washington, D.C.: Government Printing Office, 1968). Also, *Hearings before The President's National Advisory Panel on Insurance in Riot-Affected Areas, November 8 and 9, 1967* (Washington, D.C.: Government Printing Office, 1968).
[26] Foley, "The Negro Businessman: In Search of a Tradition," p. 560.
[27] See National Conference on Small Business, *Problems and Opportunities Confronting Negroes in the Field of Business,* ed. H. Naylor Fitzhugh (Washington, D.C.: Government Printing Office, 1962), p. 8.

obstacles. The argument here is twofold. First, black business is much smaller and less profitable than white business. Further, small business—white or black—will not do well and is not what the ghetto needs.

In a 1964 study of the Philadelphia black ghetto it was found that "[p]ersonal services were the most numerous, hairdressing and barbering comprising 24 percent and 11 percent, respectively, of the total number of Negroes in business. Luncheonettes and restaurants comprised 11.5 percent of the total. Many of the businesses would be submarginal if free family labor were not available. For example, median sales for a sample of Negro-owned beauty shops were $2,500, for Negro-owned luncheonettes, $6,800, and for barber shops, $4,400."[28] It seems safe to say that the 1970s will not be the decade of the small businessman. The number of black-owned businesses decreased by more than a fifth between 1950 and 1960, faster than the also declining rate for white-owned small businesses.[29] In spite of the relatively unimportant and declining role of small businesses in the economy, blacks are being encouraged to open such businesses.

Restraining potential violence seems to be the major reason for the push for black ownership. One reporter making the ghetto tour in the spring of 1969 found:

> Despite the ruins and other physical deterioration, black leaders say there is a new spirit of restraint, and perhaps a little more hope, among the people. "A community that sees itself coming into ownership of businesses and other property," said Thomas I. Atkins, Negro member of the Boston City Council, "is not anxious to destroy that which it will own."[30]

[28] Foley, "The Negro Businessman: In Search of a Tradition," p. 561. For more recent evidence see James Heilbrun, "Jobs in Harlem: A Statistical Analysis," *Regional Science Association Papers*, 1970.
[29] Eugene P. Foley, "Negroes as Entrepreneurs," in *The American Negro Reference Book*, ed. John P. Davis (Englewood Cliffs, N.J.: Prentice-Hall, 1966), p. 294.
[30] John Herbers, "Mood of the Cities: New Stakes for Blacks May Cool Things Off," *The New York Times*, April 27, 1969, Section 4, p. 8e. See also Jacob Javits, "Remarks to the 56th Annual Meeting of the U.S. Chamber of Commerce," in U.S. *Congressional Record*, 90th Cong., 2nd Sess., May 7, 1968, p. S5053.

A great effort is therefore being made to give more blacks "a piece of the action."

Helping Individual Black Businessmen

One of the major differences in the ways white middle-class communities and black ghettos are organized is in the nature of formal and informal communication and decision-making. In white communities one of the most important groups on school boards, in charity fund raising, and in other commercial undertakings is the business community. The lack of black businessmen in the ghetto deprives the community of the important contribution such groups make elsewhere. A second disadvantage in this regard is absentee ownership. As James Q. Wilson has pointed out, "Communal social controls tend to break down when persons with an interest in, and the competence for, maintaining a community no longer live in the area. . . ."[31] Resident businessmen, it is believed, add stability to their community.

The desirability of fostering the growth of small businesses has been recognized and accepted by the federal government for a long time. The Small Business Administration (SBA) makes loans to aid struggling businessmen. The extent of such aid going to blacks before the middle 1960s was minimal. A study of the ten and a half years of operation of the Philadelphia office of the SBA showed that out of 432 loans made through the fall of 1964, only seven had been to black businessmen.[32] Attempting to remedy this situation, the SBA set up a program on an experimental basis in Philadelphia to reach the "very" small businessmen, especially Negro businessmen, who operate a large segment of the very small business sector. The program involved loans up to $6,000 for six years (hence the name "6 × 6" Pilot Loan and Management Program). The SBA also offered individual training and counseling. The program was judged successful in overcoming traditional bar-

[31] James Q. Wilson, "The Urban Unease: Community vs. City," *The Public Interest*, Summer 1968, p. 34.
[32] Foley, "The Negro Businessman: in Search of a Tradition," pp. 574–575.

riers faced by black businessmen, and, to the surprise of some old-time SBA people, the delinquency rate was very low.[33]

In the late 1960s the SBA accelerated its search for qualified black borrowers, instituting special outreach programs, lowering equity requirements (which in 1968 could be less than 15 percent), guaranteeing up to 90 percent of bank loans, and developing counseling programs in cooperation with volunteer groups such as the Service Corps of Retired Executives (SCORE) and Minority Advisors for Minority Entrepreneurs (MAME).[34] In fiscal 1968 the SBA aided 2,300 minority-owned businesses with various services and promised to increase this number in years to come.[35] One thousand six hundred seventy-six minority loans were approved in fiscal 1968, about 13 percent of total SBA loans, and five percent of the total value of loans made.[36]

Unfortunately, the rapid increase in the number of loans made to minority businesses was dramatically matched with climbing loss and default rates. In fiscal 1966 the loss rate was 3.6 percent. The next year it was 8.9 percent, and in fiscal 1968 the loss rate was nearly 12 percent of loan disbursement.[37] It was hinted in the spring of 1969 that the climbing rate of losses on loans might lead to cutbacks in the SBA program.[38] Once the best prospects were helped, the economies of the more typical ghetto business had become evident. Merchants with limited capital and markets purchase on a small scale and so must charge higher prices, creating customer resentment.

One way to minimize the failure rate of new businesses is through franchising, which utilizes a "proven" product, service, and marketing technique. The franchisor usually provides location analysis, helps negotiate a lease, obtains a loan, initiates training

[33] *Ibid.*, p. 575.
[34] Small Business Administration, *Fact Sheet: Project Own* (Washington, D.C.: Small Business Administration, n.d. [received April 1969]).
[35] Allen T. Demaree, "Business Picks up the Urban Challenge," *Fortune*, April 1969, p. 176.
[36] Small Business Administration, Office of Reports, *Management Information Summary* (Washington, D.C.: Small Business Administration, May 1969), p. 25.
[37] *The New York Times*, April 21, 1969, p. 27.
[38] *Ibid.*

for the personnel, helps design and equip the store, and offers economies of centralized purchasing and advertising.[39] Franchising is also a safe way for white firms to enter the ghetto market. Franchising and the SBA programs are subject to the same criticism: small retail businesses are on the decline, and certainly to rely on small business as a way to promote black advancement in competition with white capitalism "is little more than a hoax."[40] An equally important criticism of attempts to create a greater number of black businessmen is that the economics of the ghetto may itself force the black capitalist to shortchange his "brothers," selling inferior merchandise at high prices just as other ghetto merchants do. For these reasons two other strategies seem more relevant to the economic development of the ghetto—the involvement of big business in partnership with the local community and local development corporations owned and operated by neighborhood residents.

The White Corporation in the Black Ghetto

The latter part of the 1960s witnessed the growing awareness on the part of the business community that it should become more "involved" in urban problems. Writing as a mayor of a large city with a background in business, Alfonso Cervantes stated in the fall of 1967 in the *Harvard Business Review* that before Watts he believed "businessmen should commit themselves to making money, politicians to saving the cities, do-gooders to saving the disadvantaged, and preachers to saving souls. . . . Observing the riots of Watts (and now Newark, Detroit, and other Harlems throughout the country) has converted me to an updated social orthodoxy. As a public administrator I have discovered that the economic credos of a few years ago no longer suffice; I now believe the profit motive is compatible with social rehabilitation."[41]

[39] See U.S. Department of Commerce, *Franchise Company Data for Equal Opportunity in Business* (Washington, D.C.: Government Printing Office, 1966), especially p. 4.

[40] W. Arthur Lewis, "The Road to the Top Is through Higher Education—Not Black Studies," *The New York Times Magazine*, May 11, 1969.

[41] Alfonso J. Cervantes, "To Prevent a Chain of Super Watts," *Harvard Business Review*, September–October 1967, pp. 55–56.

In a similar vein a group of corporation executives at the close of a Columbia University School of Business meeting devoted to "The Negro Challenge to the Business Community" spoke not only of the moral responsibility of business to take action, but of its self-interest in doing so. The report said, in part:

> Business cannot tolerate such disturbances. Business could be brought to a virtual standstill in such an atmosphere, as indeed it has in many parts of the world . . . the political realities are such that restrictions, legislation, and the direction of business could bring an end to what we call free enterprise.[42]

While involvement would unquestionably be of benefit to corporations as a whole, unless there is a profitable return to individual firms they will not participate.[43] The problem for government is to insure profitability through subsidies and tax incentives without allowing unearned windfall gains. As the Nixon Administration found out when it tried to make good on campaign promises, this a difficult balance to achieve.[44]

The pattern of support that has emerged in the late Johnson and early Nixon years is that an independent corporation with a name like "Opportunity Unlimited" or "Economic Resources Corporation" is set up with a predominantly black board of directors, funded by Economic Development Administration grants and loans, Labor Department training funds, and perhaps an Office of Economic Opportunity grant and Department of Housing and Urban Development assistance.[45] The key ingredient is an ongoing relation between the newly established corporation and a large established firm which supplies know-how and a long-term contract for the independent firm's output. Thus, in one well-publicized case a black group, FIGHT, in Rochester, New York,

[42] The Conference Group, "Reports of Corporate Action," in *The Negro Challenge to the Business Community*, ed. Eli Ginzberg (New York: McGraw-Hill, 1964), p. 87.
[43] Robin Marris, "Business Economics and Society," in *Social Innovation in the City: New Enterprises for Community Development*, ed. Richard S. Rosenbloom and Robin Marris (Cambridge, Mass.: Harvard University Program on Technology and Science, 1969), p. 30.
[44] *The New York Times*, May 11, 1969, p. 1.
[45] *The New York Times*, February 27, 1969, p. 1.

was assisted by Xerox in getting started. The extent of dependency in such a relationship has been described as follows:

> FIGHT's venture would have been a pipedream without the unstinting support of Xerox Corporation—from planning to production. Xerox helped to define FIGHT's product-line—metal stampings and electrical transformers. The office-copier giant will lend FIGHT two key management advisors, conduct technical training, and open the doors to bank financing. Even more important, Xerox has guaranteed to buy $1.2 million of the firm's output over a two year period.[46]

In discussing the role of Xerox in getting the Rochester firm started, another writer stated:

> Here lies one of the principal strengths of the program: a corporation often initiates a company, guarantees it a market, helps set up the business, furnishes the training, and helps iron out any start-up problems. Indeed, all the manufacturing enterprises have been established so far at the instigation of potential corporate customers.[47]

The encouragement of black entrepreneurship not only raises the income of blacks who manage the new businesses, but changes or reinforces their attitudes towards the proper methods of achieving social change. One counselor who evidently learned "a good deal from his experience" in helping a black man enter the business world, describes in the following terms the enlightened attitude of his pupil toward Negro development:

> As a leading Negro, Howard has not been fully able to accept the rebellious nature of the present civil rights movement. Certainly, he resents the forces that have limited the Negroes' development, but in many ways he rises above this. He sees himself not only as a Negro but as a member of the society of man. As the movement advances and Negroes become more educated, Howard's values may be accepted. As he says, "Education without civilization is a disaster." He expresses his indebtedness to society when he says, "Let me be recognized, let me contribute."[48]

[46] *Christian Science Monitor*, July 26, 1968.
[47] McKersie, "Vitalize Black Enterprise," p. 98.
[48] *Ibid.*, p. 96.

"Howard" would be described by some militants as an Oreo (black on the outside, white on the inside) or simply as a Tom. The achievement of such black men only reinforces the idea that blacks must struggle as individuals to escape their poverty. What is needed is not the salvation of a few but the redemption of all. This, militants argue, can be done only if all ghetto dwellers cooperatively own the economic resources of the ghetto and use these resources for the common good.

The Community Development Corporation

The contrast between those who favor aiding individual blacks or encouraging white corporations to become involved in the ghetto and those who want independent black development is not always very distinct. Current proposals being put forward in the Congress have in fact adopted the rhetoric of militancy and the trappings of the radicals' own analysis. For example, Senator Jacob Javits, addressing the U.S. Chamber of Commerce in late 1968, compared the ghetto to an emerging nation which rejects foreign domination of its economy. He suggested:

> American business has found that it must develop host country management and new forms of joint ownership in establishing plants in the fiercely nationalistic less-developed countries, [and so too] this same kind of enlightened partnership will produce the best results in the slums of our own country.[49]

In 1968 Javits along with others (including conservative Senator John Tower) proposed a bill which would establish community self-determination corporations to aid the people of urban (and rural) communities in, among other goals, "achieving the ownership and control of the resources of their community, expanding opportunity, stability, and self-determination."[50] The proposed "Community Self-Determination Act" had the support of some

[49] Javits, "Remarks to the Fifty-sixth Annual Meeting of the U.S. Chamber of Commerce," p. 5053.
[50] U.S. Congress, Senate, *Hearings on S. 3876*, 90th Cong., 2d Sess., July 24, 1968, p. S9284.

militant Black Power groups such as the Congress on Racial Equality (CORE) because it promised self-respect and independence through ownership by blacks and community control of its own development. The bill set as an important aim the restoration to the residents of local communities of the power to participate directly and meaningfully in the making of public policy decisions on issues which affect their everyday lives. "Such programs should," the bill stated, "aim to free local communities from excessive interference and control by centralized governments in which they have little or no effective voice." While the proposal was not enacted into law, it gives some indication of the type of thinking being done by influential groups and individuals. It has also directed attention to the community development concept.

Most schemes for community development corporations (CDC's) propose (1) expanding economic and educational opportunities through the purchase and management of properties and businesses; (2) improving the health, safety, and living conditions through CDC-sponsored health centers, housing projects, and so on; (3) enhancing personal dignity and independence through the expansion of opportunities for meaningful decision-making and self-determination; and (4) at the discretion of the corporation, using its profits to pay a "community dividend" rather than a return to stockholders.[51] The relation between CDC-sponsored businesses and privately owned ones is hard to delineate satisfactorily.

Some proposals suggest that the CDC should also be a development bank to make loans and grants to local businesses in order to encourage ownership. Others suggest CDC's should bond black contractors and act as a broker between ghetto residents and outside groups for government grants, franchising, and subcontracting. Such an organization would be something on the order of a central planning agency, making cost-benefit studies of business potential in different lines, keeping track of vacancies, and conducting inventories of locally available skills.[52] One study in Harlem has made "feasibility analyses," detailed cost-benefit "pro-

---

[51] *Ibid.*, pp. S927–S929.
[52] *Ibid.*, Section 110; Richard S. Rosenbloom, "Corporations for Urban Development," in Rosenbloom and Marris, *Social Innovation in the City;* and Frederick D. Sturdivant, "The Limits of Black Capitalism," *Harvard Business Review,* January–February 1969.

files," for different industries which might be developed in the ghetto. These involve a consideration of employment and income-generating potential as well as any externalities not reflected in private profit calculations.[53] After detailing the best development plan (developed by technical analysis, subject to community approval under some suitable organizational form), a development planning group would make two final measures. First, an estimate would be made of the *efficiency gaps* (the expected differences in unit operating costs between Harlem projects' activities and similar businesses already operating outside the ghetto). "These gaps will suggest the magnitude of the public subsidies necessary to complement private capital in the implementation of the plan."[54] Second, estimates would be made of needed infrastructural requirements which would "permit the Project businesses to function efficiently. This bill of requirements will then be presented to local government officials,"[55] or funded by a well-financed CDC. Under such a plan the CDC would provide social infrastructure and funds but eschew an ownership role.

Such a development bank and planning agency approach would encourage black entrepreneurship through low-cost loans and technical help. It downplays mechanisms for community control while stressing neighborhood involvement in an individual entrepreneurial role, rather than community cooperation.

The CDC schemes are expected to be financed either through stocks and bonds sold in the local community or through funding by federal agencies. Some suggest that in addition to the Neighborhood CDC's there should be a national Urban Development Corporation (UDC). The UDC, it is suggested, would not engage in development projects but could give financial and technical advice to the CDC's. The UDC would sponsor experiments and demonstration projects. A UDC could "be a source of knowledge, as well as assistance, generating new ideas for community ventures. It would develop, test, and disseminate knowledge of new means for organizing and implementing projects for creating housing, nur-

[53] Bennett Harrison, "A Pilot Project in Economic Development Planning for American Urban Slums," *International Development Review*, March 1968, p. 26.
[54] *Ibid.*, p. 27.
[55] *Ibid.*, p. 28.

turing new businesses, training the unskilled, and so forth."[56] By selective distribution of resources, based on performance measures, the UDC could increase the scale of operations of the more "effective" CDC's.[57] In this view, the CDC would be limited for funding to what it could earn and what the UDC allocated to it as a "reward for social effectiveness." Profit in the usual sense would not be the measure of efficiency.

The power relations here are subject to much debate. The idea behind the CDC is to give an organizational tool for ghetto development. The extent of control by any group outside the ghetto would in all likelihood be fought by the local leadership. Rosenbloom argues that a UDC would be needed as a "surrogate" for the market, since many CDC undertakings (day care centers, a community newspaper, health services, and so on) might not be run as profit-making ventures but are important programs worthy of financing. Through financial rewards, the UDC would recognize enterprises which improve community conditions. The danger that such controls might lead to covert or overt "manipulation" and the charges of "same old paternalism" have been recognized, but it is also pointed out that there must be an overseeing of public funds through audits and some sort of supervision.

Conflicts might also arise between CDC and powerful local interests. CDC housing rehabilitation programs might not get very much cooperation from local slumowners; buyers' cooperative stores might find local merchants using their influence to fight them; the community-run schools might have trouble reaching agreements with the city-wide board of education, the teachers' union, and so on. On the other hand, the inclusion of (white) businessmen in advisory capacities to take advantage of local expertise might be rejected by the community. The demand by the mayor and city council that they be given veto power over projects or that all money should be channeled through them would also be resisted vigorously. If poverty program experiences are indicative, militant local CDC's would find their funds cut off as political pressures of the vested interests made their power felt. The Model Cities Program has been carefully channeled through the local

[56] *Ibid.*, p. 29.
[57] Rosenbloom, "Corporations for Urban Development."

governments, and the ghetto has usually lost the battle for community control. Some of the problems involved, from the city council point of view, are shown in the vigorous resistance to giving neighborhood boards real power under Model Cities legislation.[58] This occurs partly because mayors and councilors do not like to "play second fiddle" to locally elected boards. There is a feeling that special consideration is unfair and that all parts of the city should be treated equally, and the argument that "fairness" requires restitution for past misallocation are rarely accepted by residents of the wealthier white neighborhoods. The narrow-mindedness of most local white electorates indicates that clashes between local autonomy and federal priorities may prove to be one of the more important conflicts in intergovernmental relations in the coming years.[59] Distinguishing among proposals which will encourage local control by black communities while not allowing racist policies in white neighborhoods which democratically vote to be racist is a problem that can be overcome through the application of the U.S. Constitution. It is not as difficult a task as some suggest; in fact, the suggestion that local control strengthens white bigotry, while real enough, is often stressed by those who do not want to see black communities gain real power. The inner-city blacks are asking only for the same degree of autonomy as is already enjoyed by the suburban whites who do run their police, school boards, etc. Each small town in suburbia duplicates facilities, some of which might on economic grounds be run on an area-wide basis. They do so to retain local control, even at the expense of the added financial burden.

Black Cooperation

Corporations have been criticized by some for not going far enough in terms of ghetto autonomy. Others suggest that such proposals, by going too far towards ghetto autonomy, encourage black separatism.

[58] *Ibid.*
[59] See Mahlon Apgar IV, and S. Michael Dean, "Combining Action and Research: Two Cases," in Rosenbloom and Marris, *Social Innovation in the City*, especially pp. 194–96.

The limits of black capitalism have been well stated by James Sundquist:

> Federal credit and technical assistance should be extended, and discrimination against Negro enterprises in such matters as surety bonds and other forms of insurance should be dealt with—if necessary, through federal legislation. Much can be said for a federal program to support and assist ghetto-based community development corporations that will have power to operate or finance commercial and industrial enterprises. But even with all these kinds of encouragement, to suggest that Negro entrepreneurship can produce much more than a token number of new jobs for the hard-core unemployed, at least for a long time to come, is pure romanticism. Ghetto anarchy is impossible. Even if the ghetto markets could be walled off, in effect, through appeals to Negroes to "buy black," the market is not big enough to support significant manufacturing, and the number of white employees who could be replaced by black workers in retail and service establishments is limited.[60]

For the ghetto to develop a strong "export" sector would take a great deal of expertise and capital. Both would have to be imported from outside, and for this to happen, long-standing flow patterns would have to be reversed. There are three ways this could happen.

First, private funds could be guaranteed against "expropriation" and special tax treatment given to assure profitability. The difficulty here would be that given foreign ownership, decisions would be made externally and profits could be repatriated.

Second are the proposals usually offered to help any underdeveloped nation badly in need of capital: better terms of trade and technical assistance. Foreign aid could be used to build up social overhead capital, to make investment in human capital, and to give loans to local entrepreneurs. The ghetto's one major export, unskilled labor, could be aided through a continuing national commitment to full employment. Technical assistance would include economic consultants, the establishment of research facilities to

[60] James L. Sundquist, "Jobs, Training, and Welfare for the Underclass," in *Agenda for the Nation*, ed. Kermit Gordon (Washington, D.C.: The Brookings Institution, 1968), p. 58.

study potentially profitable lines of ghetto development, and a financial commitment to pursue such avenues.

Third, if the problem is viewed as one of underdevelopment, efforts could be made to retain profits and wages of ghetto-based enterprises by demanding that those who work in the area live there. Those who hold jobs as policemen, teachers, postal employees, clerks, or small businessmen would have a greater interest in "their" community if they lived in it. Cooperative forms of ownership would also lead to greater community control and to a greater retention of capital in the ghetto.

The timing and the substance of the gains blacks make will be determined by whether they rely primarily on aid from the corporate sector and the government or instead organize locally to control their own economy. Self-development implies organizational strength, a will and an ability to fight for political power. Thus Barry Bluestone has argued that

> while the creation of a black economy in the ghetto may not lead inexorably to a viable economic base—competitive with the staunchest of white enterprise—the act of striving toward an inner city economy yields a powerful tool for organizing the black community into a coherent political force capable of extracting concessions on jobs, housing, income, and dignity from the government and from the corporate establishment. While black socialism alone may not be capable of rooting out poverty, it may root out powerlessness and thus gain for the black community the indirect means to freedom from poverty and the manifestations of racism. In the striving for economic independence, not only is dependence on the white power structure for jobs and poverty incomes reduced, but the economic incentive to coalesce within the black community increases as well. Jobs and income are created within the community and it is from such a base that political and social power are born.[61]

There is evidence that important sections of the black community hold views similar to those of Bluestone.

In the spring of 1969 when the Thirty-fifth American Assembly decided to devote its attention to "Black Capitalism," a sounding

---

[61] Barry Bluestone, "Black Capitalism: The Path to Black Liberation?" *The Review of Radical Economics* (Ann Arbor, Mich.: Union for Radical Political Economics, May 1969), p. 53.

of the invited black participants persuaded sponsors to change the conference name to "Black Economic Development." "We do not want parity in the present system," one of the young black participants explained; "our goal is not simply to get a greater share in what already exists. . . . We want a new concept of American economic organization."[62] Black business, participants stressed, should function to serve blacks. This principle was illustrated by the example of a Harlem investment group which "weighed the relative merits of a computer type industry and an all night drugstore and decided on the all night drug store because of the community need for one."[63] Another conference participant spoke of the need for opportunity for blacks like that given to the farmer, the oil industry, and the railroads—i.e., subsidies.[64]

Dick Gregory has expressed similar views:

> What is needed is a concept of black cooperativism. Black capitalism as it is currently understood means a few individuals establishing a business to make a profit. The development of cooperative businesses allows many black people to work for profit and survival. It is cooperativism, rather than capitalism, which stands a chance of ending the current paternalistic overtones of federal programs.[65]

The argument for community control stems from two lines of analysis. First, white society may be scared by riots into making some concessions, but this is a costly strategy both in terms of loss of black lives and liberties and because of the strengthening of anti-black feelings among large numbers of whites. Second, there is the view that development by outsiders takes out of the hands of the community the control over extent and speed of development. In this light the purpose of black capitalism schemes seems to be to prevent future urban guerrilla warfare. In spite of the large amount of publicity so far, very few blacks have benefited. It appears that the programs are meant to do little more than "cool things" by making promises and calling for more patience.

[62] *The New York Times*, April 27, 1969, p. 62.
[63] *Ibid.*
[64] *Ibid.*
[65] Dick Gregory, "Black Capitalism or Black Cooperativism," *Connecticut Daily Campus*, February 5, 1969.

There is also the fear that if black capitalism works, the ghetto will turn inward, in attempts to build a corner-store capitalism, rather than outward in attempts at restructuring economic goals and societal allocation of resources. The success of black businessmen in the ghetto could remove one source of tension without significantly altering the conditions of most blacks.

A more demanding stance would call for massive federal funds to make investments in deteriorated public facilities, community control of the economic base through cooperative forms of ownership, neighborhood control of local public institutions, and, finally, the demand for production for use. Demands for such changes could have a major impact on the larger society's future development. Community control or black cooperativism is, in itself, not a complete statement of this demand, much less a strategy for its attainment. But, as an alternative to individual black capitalism, it is a proposal which points away from neo-colonial control over the ghetto, rather than a strengthening of that control. Robert Allen has written:

> . . . any black capitalist or managerial class must act, in effect, as the tacit representative of the white corporations which are sponsoring that class. The task of this class is to ease corporate penetration of the black communities and facilitate corporate planning and programming of the markets and human resources in those communities. This process occurs regardless of the personal motivations of the individuals involved, because it stems from the nature of the corporate economy itself and the dependent status of the fledgling, black capitalist-managerial class.[66]

The strategy of some militants, especially those identified with CORE, has been to go to the business sector for assistance. They, after all, are the people with the money. From subsidizing individual black businessmen it is a small step to encouraging large outside firms to enter the ghetto on favorable terms. If economic development is viewed in a non-political context, this may appear to be a sensible strategy. However, if accepted, such an approach will prove costly both to the taxpayer and in terms of black autonomy. These matters will be argued at length in the following chapter.

[66] Robert L. Allen, *Black Awakening in Capitalist America: An Analytic History* (Garden City, N.Y.: Doubleday, 1969), pp. 187–88.

CHAPTER 4

Location Subsidies and Corporate Involvement

During the 1968 presidential campaign, candidate Richard Nixon spoke about black capitalism as a means of giving ghetto residents "a piece of the action." His suggestions, certainly consistent with the Moynihan strategy discussed in Chapter 1, were met with favor by important elements in big business and the black community. Business saw both financial and public relations value in the plan. Blacks sensed that if given the incentive of potential profit, business could make a substantial impact on ghetto growth.

As American capitalism matures into the "New Industrial State," in which stability and dependable estimates of the future become important requisites for long-term success, the citizen is valued by the corporation not only as a worker but as a consumer. It may also be that, for some large corporations, crude racism may be becoming objectively less useful and in significant ways harmful to their interests. This is, however, far from a simple matter. There are contradictory needs. Cheap labor is still essential. Even oligopolistic producers try to squeeze more profits out of their workers through assembly line speed-ups and by changing job categories to downgrade wage scales. What has changed dramatically is the cost of keeping black workers in the marginal role of a low-wage buffer pool. The very size of the black population, combined with decreasing need for low-skilled labor, and the social costs of perpetuating segregation and discrimination work to decrease the corporate sector's support for the American caste system. Some modifications are called for in the corporate sector's self-interest. At a time when the dangers of urban rebellion are great indeed, black purchasing power has become important to the business firm. These trends reinforce one another and have guaranteed business interest in the ghetto.

"Potentially," Sumner Myers writes in the *Harvard Business Review,* "cities are one of the richest markets for new products and systems of products produced by business. To date, however, most companies have been generally frustrated in their efforts to sell innovative ideas to the cities."[1] These efforts have failed because businessmen have encountered difficulties in marketing to the many relatively small, scattered potential urban consumer groups. The cities obviously have problems, such as congestion, pollution, and so on. Most important are the issues of safety and crime, which affect individuals and property owners and, on the larger scale, contribute to the breakdown of voluntary cooperation with authority and the legitimacy of social institutions, which command increasingly less respect.

These issues are felt most strongly in the central city. One way to cope with them is to re-allocate resources to the core areas in order to re-establish loyalties and a sense of belonging. The corporate sector stands ready to do this. From its point of view, what is needed is larger purchasing units with money to buy. The federal government or large quasi-public urban development corporations could serve this function.

Corporations have started to involve themselves to a limited extent; an example is the demonstration program, such as the efforts in education: Xerox in teaching machines, IBM in computerized classrooms, and CBS in classroom uses of television. Government expenditures on such programs have proved acceptable to fiscal conservatives. How can such efforts be encouraged and broadened in scope? Myers asks: "By what means can companies be induced

[1] Sumner Myers, "How to Sell New Ideas to the Cities," *Harvard Business Review*, July–August 1968, p. 111.

to take part in a system that performs a socially desirable function?"[2] The answer, of course, is money. Now is the time to provide these corporations with the same guaranteed profits they have come to enjoy in the space and defense industries. If businesses make profits, they will work for the public good. Or so it is argued.

Others have urged involvement out of even more narrow corporate self-interest. "In 1966," the president of Illinois Bell Telephone writes, "protests and demonstrations racked Chicago as the Reverend Martin Luther King, Jr., led his followers through the streets of the city in their demand for open housing. The demonstrators had the power to disrupt, even to destroy."[3] A group of businessmen, realizing that "the situation was desperate,"[4] formed a leadership council to find solutions to the housing problems of minority groups. The telephone company president, Mr. Cook, felt he had good reason to accept the chairmanship of the group. "More than 75 percent of the company's investment of roughly $2.5 billion is within thirty-five or forty miles of our downtown headquarters building. Unlike many other businesses we cannot pull up stakes and move away."[5]

Until recently corporate involvement has occurred on this basis —as an ad hoc group of local corporate executives and community leaders—the most publicized of these being the Urban Coalition and the New Detroit Committee.[6] Increasingly, however, poverty-area redevelopment will be attempted more systematically by large urban development corporations like the one which was set up in New York State under the sponsorship of Governor Rockefeller. Such an organization has extensive powers to override local sovereignty. "The new managers of the ghetto," Cloward and Piven have suggested, "will be huge quasi-public development cor-

---

[2] *Ibid.*, p. 112.
[3] James W. Cook, "Why a Company Gets Involved," *Bell Telephone Magazine*, March–April 1969, p. 12.
[4] *Ibid.*
[5] *Ibid.* Also see *Action Report*, a digest of corporate approaches to public problems published by the Chase Manhattan Bank. Its descriptions of which firms are involved in helping to solve the "urban crisis" (how and why) makes interesting reading.
[6] The cliché-ridden *Report of the New Detroit Committee* (privately printed, undated) is also a good example of the product of such groups.

porations (like the New York Port Authority) insulated from effective political control and endowed with powers to issue bonds, condemn property, and form webs of relations with private investment companies . . ."[7]

This approach can be criticized as elitist. The social-industrial complex may prove just as wastefully expensive as its defense counterpart, and equally beyond democratic control. Corporations which have assiduously avoided responsibility for the social costs of their own actions are now being given subsidies to rebuild our public environment.

One program for corporate involvement which has been advanced is the payment of incentives to firms which will locate plants in urban poverty areas. This approach is advocated by those who favor economic development of the ghetto through a primary reliance on the private market. The idea is to influence company decision-makers, through subsidies and tax credits, to locate in close proximity to low-income residential areas, thus minimizing transportation difficulties and simplifying job-seeking. The large corporations have know-how and financial strength which locally-run firms, privately or cooperatively owned, cannot be expected to have. Therefore, if large numbers of jobs for ghetto residents are to be found, they will have to be created in the "white" economy.

The location incentive approach is discussed extensively in this chapter because it is the tactic most likely to receive congressional blessing. It is fully within the American tradition of generously subsidizing the private sector to carry out socially desirable policies which it would not otherwise be inclined to do. The lack of close correspondence between measurable and non-measurable benefits received and costs paid by all groups involved (including, of course, taxpayers) under such plans is unfortunately also within the tradition of past experiences with incentive schemes.

The policy questions to be answered in discussing this approach are whether outside firms can be induced to locate in urban poverty areas, and, if so, whether this is a constructive policy. The first of these can be divided into a series of smaller questions: What

[7] Richard A. Cloward and Francis Fox Piven, "Ghetto Redevelopment: Corporate Imperialism for the Poor," *The Nation*, October 16, 1967, p. 366.

factors influence the industrial location decision-making process at the regional, community, and site levels of analysis? What incentives are needed to attract firms to urban poverty areas? What types of firms are most likely to respond to such inducements? The second major question divides into technical concerns such as the impact of firm location on employment opportunities in the area, expenditure patterns, effects on the stability of the neighborhood, and the costs of the incentive program as against alternative methods of job creation. All these questions relate to the way market forces allocate economic activity in the urban environment.

Factors Influencing Industrial Location

Our knowledge of the factors which influence locational decisions is not as complete as we might like, and the uniqueness of each decision makes generalization hazardous. Still, from available evidence, there seem to be six major factors influencing industrial location: land costs, local tax policies, the location of the firm's markets, the transfer cost structure, the local labor market characteristics, and the possible external economics. The first two are amenable to influence by government. The final four are, in the short run at least, beyond the direct reach of policy-makers.

Transport—or transfer costs, as the location economists would term them—depend upon resource and market location. For example, the necessity of face-to-face contact with customers and legal and financial services might favor a central-city location. Labor market considerations may favor the South as a region when low-wage labor is sought. Cambridge, Massachusetts, or some other "university town" may be preferred if access to high-level brain power is essential. Site choice will be influenced, too, by labor-force requirements. Low-wage labor will not be as able, or perhaps not be willing, to commute to outlying parts of the metropolitan area, while suburban higher-income workers may prefer such plant locations.

These five factors have interacted to produce three discernible trends in the postwar period. First, there has been a spreading out, a decentralization of economic activity among the regions of the nation. Second, there has been a tendency for the middle-size cities to grow faster than the largest-size group. Third, there has been a tendency for suburban locations to be favored over central-city locations. This last trend is perhaps the most significant in considering the plight of urban subemployed, although the other two have had a strong influence. All three are the direct result of important market factors. Population shifts and the search for lower labor costs have contributed to the spreading out of economic activity. The desire to escape large-city problems while maintaining an urban location in part explains the faster growth of middle-size cities. The favoring of suburban locations appears to be the result of the preference for using large tracts of land for plant construction, avoidance of the increasing traffic congestion, and a desire for more "pleasant" surroundings.[8] It may in fact be that the urban core area has lost its centrality, its claim to being the most valued location.

The inner cities have, consequently, felt the tight pinch of declining industrial employment opportunities.[9] The response has been pressure to help the central cities. One source of this pressure has been elected representatives of these areas, who are pressed by recognized community leadership groups; pressure has also resulted from national awareness of potentially explosive situations—as well as from the experience of actual outbreaks of violence in the central cities.

Those academic scholars and government policy-makers who favor federal action in the form of incentives for firms locating in urban poverty areas rely on three interrelated economic arguments: the infant industry analogy, the spread effects, and the wasted worker thesis. Each of these arguments will now be considered in turn.

[8] U.S. Department of Commerce, Economic Development Administration, *Industrial Location As a Factor in Regional Economic Development* (Washington, D.C.: Government Printing Office, 1967).
[9] Between 1954 and 1965 almost two-thirds of all new industrial buildings (measured by valuation) . . . were constructed outside the nation's central cities. . . . Between 1947 and 1967, total employment in seven large central cities rose only 50,000 while employment in the metropolitan rings surrounding those same cities increased by 900,000." U.S. Department of Labor, *A Report on Manpower Requirements, Resources, Utilization, and Training* (Washington, D.C.: Government Printing Office, 1967), p. 87.

Theoretical Arguments for Location Incentives

The infant industry position can be stated in terms of the familiar model of two regions which begin at some point in time to trade freely. One region is characterized by an advanced technology, a large internal market, long production experience, and economies of scale in production. This first region is able to undersell the second even in the latter's home market. The argument is advanced that it is in the second region's interests to subsidize the development of its own industry, which will, of necessity, operate initially at a disadvantage. However, once it overcomes its inexperience, adequately trains its labor force, and builds up sales volume, it will be self-sustaining, able to compete effectively. Similarly for a declining region: once it overcomes its original disadvantages, industry in the poverty area will become competitive.

The spread effect argument goes farther in this direction. Its proponents reason that the new industries train the local labor force, show that the workers of the area are potentially more productive than was hitherto thought, and in general by their example encourage other industries to emulate them and locate in similar areas. Through their consumption expenditures in the local market, the newly employed workers provide jobs for others. The firm itself will buy services locally. Suppliers will be induced to locate nearby. Thus the effects on the surrounding region are assumed to be sizable inasmuch as an initial subsidy pays substantial dividends—jobs, tax revenues, and new goods and services generated.

This general line of reasoning ignores some crucial differences between underdeveloped and relatively closed nation-states on the one hand, and the depressed sections of the city located in close proximity to the growth areas of the metropolis on the other. Urban poverty areas cannot be considered regions isolated from their surroundings, as the analogy to the two-nation model suggests, in the important respect that capital and goods cannot be prevented from flowing between the two regions. There is no direct correlation, for example, between industry growth rate or return to stockholders and growth of regional per capita income induced by industrial location. The region cannot place nationalistic development constraints on "foreign" capital. But more important, the urban poverty area is simply not a closed region. The disadvantages of being an internal colony preclude the possibility of autonomous development.

Spread effects are limited, because of the minor importance of internal linkages within the urban poverty area. The area can supply little of the materials or machinery needed by its factories. Moreover, most of the wide market served by the firm is located outside the poverty area; therefore, the linkages between the firm and potential customers within the region are also weak. Export industries do not generate much in the way of service activities within the area itself, since firms draw on the wider metropolitan region. All types of consumption leakages from the region tend to be high, as people buy outside the neighborhood. As a result, spread effects through secondary income generation are not great.

The test of the incentive-to-locate approach lies not only in the ability of the subsidized industry to generate income directly, but in its indirect impact upon the area in terms of backward linkages: derived demand for services, office supplies, legal aid, materials for inputs into the productive process and their induced income effect, the increased consumption out of income spent locally. Finally, there is the impact of any forward linkages leading to the location of customers in the same region.[10] Such spread effect will increase with the size of the area; but, of course, as a larger area is considered, the impact on those who live in the hard-core poverty area diminishes.

A third rationale for the location incentive approach depends on the following line of argument: living patterns, industrial location, and transportation costs in our large urban areas conspire against potential workers, so that their skills are wasted. The high costs of commuting prevent most urban poor from working in distant parts of the metropolitan area.[11] This "immobility" also results from a

[10] See Edward L. Ullman, "The Basic-Service Ratio and the Area Support of Cities," in *The Community Economic Base and Multiplier*, ed. E. Z. Palmer (Lincoln, Neb.: University of Nebraska Press, 1958).

[11] For example, it costs $40 a month to commute by public transportation from Harlem to aircraft factories on Long Island. See U.S. Department of Labor, *A Report on Manpower Requirements, Resources, Utilization, and Training*, p. 87.

psychological block harbored by the disadvantaged workers, rendering them incapable of holding or even seeking jobs in areas where employment opportunities exist.[12] Assume for a moment, however, that minority-group wage rates at jobs in suburban plants are close to those enjoyed by white workers already working in those plants. The phenomenon of reverse commuting seems to give some credence to the view that workers in the urban poverty areas do in fact travel to industrial jobs in suburban areas. An alternative hypothesis that might be considered is that the "disadvantaged" workers qualify in the main for low-paying jobs, and their pay scale does not compensate for the cost of taking high-cost transportation (car) or three changes of subway trains and then a bus. There are also problems in convincing minority-group workers that jobs are open to them in suburban plants. In any case, it is argued by some, since meaningful integration must await education over generations and the gradual change of attitudes, inducing private industry to locate in urban poverty areas offers an alternative means of helping to alleviate the problems in such areas. It is questionable, however, whether locating new industrial activity in the urban poverty area would help end its isolation, bring it back into contact with the larger society, and "develop a sense of joint community of achievement and purpose."[13] Finally, according to the Bureau of the Census classifications developed for the Office of Economic Opportunity (OEO), there are currently 193 designated poverty areas in 100 Standard Metropolitan Statistical Areas (SMSA's). Three districts, identified on the basis of education, income, housing, etc., contain about 22 percent of the census tracts in these SMSA's.[14] While there were half a million people unem-

[12] Willard Wirtz, testifying at hearings on the federal role in urban affairs, went so far as to say: "Most of the unemployed in the slums don't want to go more than six or eight blocks away from their homes. They are ... conditioned by a century of insecurity which creates a very real problem the minute a job emerges more than six or eight blocks away from where they live." Cited in Robert F. Kennedy, "Memorandum on Industrial Development Legislation," undated staff release, mimeo.
[13] Robert F. Kennedy, "Remarks Introducing a Bill for Industrial Investment in Urban Poverty Areas," *Congressional Record*, July 12, 1967, Vol. 113, Part 14, pp. 18443–18448.
[14] See U.S. Bureau of the Census, *1960 Census of Population, Supplementary Reports*, PC (S1) 69–54 (Washington, D.C.: Government Printing Office, November 13, 1967).

ployed in these designated poverty areas (as of March 1966), they represented "only" seven and one-half percent of the areas' work force. These statistics are important for two reasons. First, there are many gainfully employed yet poor residents in these designated areas who are employed at very low pay scales and hence are still in poverty or close to it. These people need help in upgrading their skills, and so indiscriminate subsidies which do not take into account the quality of job created might not help this group. Second, many of the people in the poverty areas are not "poor." For these people to be given newly created jobs would also be to miss the target group. These shortcomings are mentioned not to suggest that new jobs created in the urban poverty area would not be useful, but rather to argue that the gains in terms of the objectives of the program would not be as great as might at first blush be hoped.

These three lines of argument—the infant industry analogy and the spread effects and wasted worker theses—while not convincing in themselves, can be woven into a more complete model of underdevelopment which some may find convincing. It is to such a model that we now turn. Both the arguments to be offered for the approach and the program of corporate involvement itself implicitly assume the unimportance and inefficiency of the community ownership approach discussed in Chapter 3.

The Location Incentive Approach

The strategy implicit in the location incentive approach seems to be based upon an analysis of the urban poverty situation which might be summarized in the following terms. Overall investment tax credits and accelerated depreciation allowances are not by their nature selective enough to create jobs for the hard-core unemployed and, more generally, those with poor labor-force participation experience. Training programs, since they are limited to filling available job openings, still leave the poor potentially without work, even after training, or increase the competition for scarce jobs. Therefore, stress should be placed upon the creation of new jobs for the subemployed poor. Since ghetto residents are loath to seek jobs at any distance from their homes, it is further argued, the location of job opportunities within the ghetto is of prime importance to the residents of urban poverty areas.[15]

Manpower strategists seem to be in agreement that job creation should be undertaken in such a way as to utilize fully the potential skills of members of the labor force at the lowest possible cost per job. A locational incentive program might well subsidize sweatshops with their dead-end offerings, or induce the location of highly capital-intensive plants creating few jobs at a high cost per job. Some firms will receive windfall gains to locate where they would have located in the absence of the legislation. And, of course, much depends on the area in question. East Harlem is already industrial and is still poor.

Bringing industrial activity into urban poverty areas may also be expected to have adverse effects upon both the neighborhood and its residents. The questions which must be asked are: Do we really want to concentrate the ghetto any further? Do we expect ghetto residents to be pleased at having to relocate so that factories can be built where their homes now stand? Do we expect their neighbors to appreciate living in close proximity to factories? Would a mixed industrial-residential area improve a neighborhood or accelerate its decay? We cannot attempt answers to these complex questions here. We shall, however, speak to the more particular effects of such a program on employment in the urban poverty area, and the monetary costs of the jobs created. We shall ask: What kinds of jobs would be created under the proposed locational incentive program, who will get these jobs, what will the cost be per job, and what secondary effects can be expected?

A Proposal

Answers to the above questions can be given only in conjunction with a consideration of a particular program. One such plan which

[15] It might also be argued that within the ghetto the economic units with lowest earning potential (those headed by women and aged) are increasing, while those with young male heads are decreasing, and therefore, locating industry that would tie employed minority-group men to the ghetto would have a positive neighborhood effect. For evidence of worsening conditions since 1960 in the ghetto of one major city, see Walter Williams, "Cleveland's Crisis Ghetto," *Trans-Action*, September 1967.

has received widespread attention is a bill submitted in 1967 by the late Senator Robert Kennedy. The objective of the Kennedy bill (S. 2088) is to create a "New Partnership Against Poverty" between private enterprise and government to stimulate investment which will create new jobs and additional income for the poorer residents of urban areas.[16] The proposed act enumerates various forms of assistance to be provided by the government to firms which, by meeting a series of specified requirements, qualify for aid. The law as proposed would operate in the following manner: a firm requesting certification by the secretary of Housing and Urban Development must (1) hire a minimum of fifty workers, two-thirds of whom must be low-income persons from among the residents of the urban poverty area, or persons from among the generally available unemployed, (2) not be a competitor in the local market (market being congruent with the urban poverty area as defined in the bill), (3) remunerate workers at rates not less than the amended Walsh-Healy minimum wage, nor below the prevailing minimum wages for persons doing similar work in localities where any such facility is located, and (4) keep careful records to enable the secretary to ensure compliance with the provisions of the act.

In exchange, the certified employer is eligible for (1) a seven-percent tax credit on expenditures for constructing an industrial facility or leasing space for a qualifying business, (2) a ten-percent credit on machinery and equipment, (3) a carryback credit of three taxable years, (4) a credit carryover of ten taxable years, (5) a net operating loss carryover of ten taxable years, (6) accelerated depreciation of 66 2/3 percent of the normal useful life applicable to real and personal property for tax purposes, (7) a tax deduction of 25 percent of the salaries paid to workers hired under the second requirement listed above, and (8) training allowances for the workers hired.

The bill also provides for the recovery of all credits if the firm does not hold to the provisions of the act. It safeguards local residents of the poverty area by stipulating that public hearings will precede the issuance of certificates, and that the local governing

[16] Robert F. Kennedy, "Remarks Introducing a Bill for Industrial Investment in Urban Poverty Areas."

body of the city must first give written notice of a desire to participate in the program. "Runaway" corporations would not qualify. All jobs created must be new employment. In addition, allowances for relocation of households and businesses are provided, along with provisions for retraining of subsidized workers.

After a consideration of the bill's major provisions, the first question that logically arises is: Would anybody be interested in these incentives, and, if so, who? A second question would be: What types of jobs would potential employers create for the urban subemployed they might be induced to hire?

Prospective Employers and the Labor-Capital "Mix"

One good indication of which firms might be induced to locate in the central city can be found by considering the types of firms which are currently located there. A second approach would be to look at the kinds of companies which have taken an interest in these areas in recent years. The third approach would be to start by looking at the industries having characteristics which might be attracted by the particular provisions of the proposed bill.

It should be evident that large manufacturing firms, if for no other reason than their land needs, will not be induced to locate in urban proverty areas. The few with plants in such areas have been there for some time. New manufacturing plants are not to be found in urban poverty areas. Rather, the businesses that are there are light manufacturing, warehouses, service companies, some office buildings, firms connected with wholesale distribution and retail companies. These firms tend to be either smaller undertakings than similar businesses located elsewhere, or branches of large firms wishing to sell to the neighborhood market. There is little export activity, aside from labor services to other parts of the metropolitan area. Expansion of such market-oriented businesses is not promising.

In recent years there has been an increase in the number of large, outside companies setting up branch plants which manufacture products for the "export" market. Most of these undertakings—such as The Watts Manufacturing Company set up by Aerojet-General, and Avco's printing plant in Boston's Roxbury section—have been subsidized by government funds, usually through training subsidies. The firms which have responded to existing government programs are in general very large, well-established firms which can risk heavy losses in such operations (Xerox, IBM, General Electric, etc.). Avco's experience has been that, even with training subsidies averaging $4,950 per man, they are unable to recoup the indirect costs of hiring the hard-core unemployed. Avco, in addition, by contracting with a consortium of black builders (which it helped organize) to construct a new plant, paid approximately 20 percent more than if the job had been done through open bidding, and paid land costs estimated at four times that of suitable suburban industrial locations.[17] In addition to large firms which have invested in urban poverty areas because of either feelings of corporate social responsibility or desire for favorable publicity, there have been firms induced by two other incentives to become involved in urban poverty areas. First, there have been firms seeking to create a long-run market for their products (Alcoa's and U.S. Gypsum's involvement, for example, seem to be of this nature), or industrial firms like Warner and Swazey, who have a plant located in the Hough district of Cleveland where they are exposed to ghetto violence. Such firms are primarily interested in protecting their investments. Unfortunately, the role of private enterprise has, generally speaking, been limited to these special cases.[18] A more fruitful approach might be for government to assume benefits at a level which will induce firms to locate, and ask the firm what types of jobs are likely to be created through the subsidy plan and who would be likely to receive the jobs that are created. We shall consider three types of firms: a capital-intensive firm, a firm with an "average" capital-labor ratio, and a labor-intensive firm, and discuss the possible outcome of subsidizing them to locate in urban poverty areas.

It may well be that a highly capital-intensive plant will find location-inducing incentives attractive. Such a plant, however, is likely

---

[17] *Christian Science Monitor*, July 19, 1968.
[18] Joel B. Hincks, "The Role of Private Enterprise in the Solution of Major Urban Problems" (Washington, D.C.: Library of Congress Legislative Reference Service, November 30, 1967) for a dated but good coverage of some of the firms involved in such projects.

to require two classes of employees: janitors and high-paid workers. The laborer in the second class would be "a skilled watchman of control panels, with duties demanding patience, alertness to malfunctioning, and a sense of responsibility for costly equipment."[19] These are hardly the characteristics of the typical unemployed poverty-area resident. Such an outcome suggests that subsidizing capital will further accentuate the distance between the disadvantaged worker and the requirements of a large number of the available jobs. Studies of firms which have located in labor-surplus areas support this view. Somers, for example, in his study of a firm opening a plant in West Virginia, found:

> Unemployed and underemployed workers would constitute an important source of labor. Such workers would be plentiful in a depressed area, but this survey indicates that they would not constitute the most important source of labor for a high-wage firm of good reputation and rigorous hiring standards.[20]

Most of those hired in the plant studied were, in any case, not unemployed; they quit other jobs to work in the new plant. Most "good" positions were held by persons who came from outside the region.[21]

In firms not characterized by a preponderance of either high- or low-wage employees, the effect of poverty-area location on upper-income workers must be given serious attention. Will skilled employees be comfortable working in neighborhoods where other racial or ethnic groups predominate? Will managerial personnel willingly take assignments in the proposed plant? If availability of cheap labor is not of primary importance, the locational disadvantages may be overwhelming. Possibly the subsidy provisions for new plant and equipment and the accelerated depreciation may induce location, but such provisions, if they weigh heavily enough to induce location, will also be sufficiently important to bias the production function in favor of greater capital intensity. This is

[19] U.S. Department of Labor, *Manpower Report of the President* (Washington, D.C.: Government Printing Office, 1966), p. 15.
[20] G. Somers, "Labor Recruitment in a Depressed Rural Area," *Monthly Labor Review*, October 1958, p. 1120.
[21] *Ibid.*, p. 1117.

especially true when the lower productivity of workers who would be attracted to plants located in poverty areas is also taken into account.

New jobs for urban poverty-area residents can also come from the location of industries mainly seeking a low-wage work force. The problem here is that such industries have found it cheaper to locate in low-wage, low-cost-of-living, labor-surplus areas (primarily in the South), rather than low-wage, high-cost-of-living, labor-surplus areas. This problem is due, in the former case, to regional attachment by the worker and to the lower cost of living, which conspire with the employer to keep wages low. The lack of unionization in the region tends to perpetuate the low-wage pattern, while local governments, more concerned with job creation and the tax base, discourage organizing attempts. Wages in urban poverty areas, low as they may be, are still higher than in rural areas, because of the economic reality of high rents, food costs, and high payments to credit merchants. Since many of the existing wage differences between regions are greater than the subsidies suggested in S. 2088, it would seem that the wage allowance provision will not have great incentive effect—especially when one considers the lower limits imposed by the Kennedy bill.[22]

If the object of social policy is to help a particular area, attention must be directed to the *types* of industries which might find the area potentially attractive. The social planner must be concerned with discovering, first, what sort of economic activity will offer the residents stable employment at adequate wages, and, second, what industries can be attracted at lowest costs from among a list of desirable ones. Any less specific formulation of the issue leaves open the possibility of attracting undesirable industries—marginal undertakings made possible by the favored treatment, which are unlikely candidates for long-run, smooth functioning without continual subsidies—or industries that cost much to attract but offer little employment to the residents of the region.

[22] On the question of the effects of wage differences in inducing shifts in industrial location within the New York metropolitan region, the results of at least one major study support the conclusion that it is "doubtful" that wage differences will play much of a role. See Edgar M. Hoover and Raymond Vernon, *Anatomy of a Metropolis* (Cambridge, Mass.: Harvard University Press, 1959).

The major difficulty that emerges from the discussion of the incentive program thus far is that such a program works against strong market forces in a socially costly manner. The proposal calls for a non-optimal spatial allocation of resources by subsidizing firms indiscriminately, thus offering pecuniary gains to many firms that may not be desired and to others which need not act any differently than they would in the absence of the subsidy. The proposal does little to change the factors which make central city locations inferior to suburban sites, i.e., traffic congestion, site cost, unattractive surroundings, etc. Nor does the proposal come to grips with the possibility that perhaps the market evaluation of the situation is accurate and that if the concern is with the urban subemployed, direct concern with that group of people should be the focal point of government programs.

The appeal to the profit motive should be invoked not ritualistically, but rather because there are times when working with the market has inherent advantages. Where subsidies aim at influencing decisions, care must be taken to limit the amount of the subsidy to the minimum necessary to achieve its aim. If job creation is desired, one type of subsidy is appropriate (i.e., investment credits, accelerated depreciation allowances, lower interest rates, etc.). But if the aim is to place disadvantaged workers in decently paying jobs, the strategy should be to make the hiring of these workers advantageous to industry (i.e., through wage subsidies, training allowances, etc.), or to make such hiring a provisional necessity in government contracts (as is done with the use of anti-discrimination clauses). Incentives for location should subsidize selectively to achieve their specific purpose and help to overcome specific locational problems (e.g., higher insurance, land and transportation costs). There is much to be learned in this regard from experience in development planning. It may well be that some combination of investment in social overhead capital—better transportation to inner city locations, for example, combined with government-subsidized insurance schemes—might induce certain types of industries to reconsider an urban poverty-area site. An attempt would have to be made to identify firms potentially interested in such locations, and to see what types of incentives it would take to induce location. Tax rebates might turn out not to be very attractive to many of these firms; but insurance, low-cost long-term loans, help in assembling a site, training subsidies—such incentives, either singly or in some combination, might prove important. This type of analysis, based on the particular land-use, income-expenditure patterns, and labor-force characteristics of the area on the one hand; and on the identification of potentially promising business undertakings on the other, is at the heart of such projects as the OEO-sponsored "Demonstration Economic Development Program for Harlem."[23] Such an analysis of the poverty area, while time-consuming and costly, might prove in the long run to bring better results and a greater benefit-cost ratio of funds committed under any resulting subsidy program.

Summary and Alternative Proposals

Industrial location incentives have been proposed with the view in mind of creating new jobs for the unemployed. If the assumption of relative immobility on the part of the target group is dropped, the task of public policy may be stated in terms of job creation for this group, the urban subemployed. It is assumed that those unable to work will be reached through some form of income mainte-nance (the form might vary from proposals such as the negative income tax to an upgraded welfare system). This class of assist-ance is not an alternative to job creation for those willing, able, and preferring to work. The different proposals which have been put forward to help the urban subemployed get and hold jobs are both alternative and complementary to the location incentive ap-proach. They will be discussed under Chapter 6.

When the underemployed and the labor-market dropouts are added to the large number of unemployed in the poverty areas, the resulting total of persons needing jobs is assuredly too large to be accommodated under even the most hopeful estimates of new plant locations.

The real question, of course, is whether such programs can be-

[23] See Bennett Harrison, "A Pilot Project in Economic Development Plan-ning for American Urban Slums," *International Development Review*, March 1968.

gin to solve ghetto income and employment problems. The answer, after all the analysis is over, is still no. Such measures are simply too ineffectual in countering basic discriminatory patterns in the labor market and too weak to overcome widespread poverty.[24] Focusing policy on location incentive also neglects the more important need for open access to the better jobs which are becoming available in suburban locations. Breaking down hiring and housing discrimination and maintaining full employment are more to the point than subsidizing firms to come back to central cities which they have left out of economic necessity. The question that must be faced is why the ghetto is kept apart from the larger society, why black people are isolated and live at economic levels little better than half as high as those enjoyed by whites. The discussions of poverty and job markets in the next two chapters deal with this question.

[24] William K. Tabb, "Government Incentives to Locate in Urban Poverty Areas" *Land Economics*, November 1969.

CHAPTER 5

Urban Poverty
and Public Policy

The previous chapters show the difficulties in solving the problems of the ghetto by currently proposed means. Even if there is some success in enlarging the black middle class, there will continue to be poor and dependent people in the ghetto. In Chapter 1, in fact, it was suggested that this group becomes relatively worse off over time. In this chapter the nature of poverty is discussed.

To best understand the underdevelopment of the black ghetto, it is useful to view poverty as lack of freedom and absence of choice. Poverty in this light is not merely low income. It is degradation as a result of dependence. Dependence would be degrading even if consumption levels of welfare were not far below those of the "non-poor." To view poverty as dependence is to see the poor, and especially the nonwhite poor, as a class set apart. Consider, for example, the way assistance is provided for those in poverty. Many who are poor receive health care in government-sponsored clinics, housing in public projects, sustenance through food stamps, and income from welfare payments. What is given is very limited and offered grudgingly. Services provided are minimal, and the stigma of charity is integral to the relationship between giver and receiver.

To say that lack of freedom is an important element in being poor is to argue not merely that because of low income the poor lack command over goods and services; it is to say also that the poor have less choice as to where and how they will live, how their children will be educated, the occupation they will find.

These twin themes—poverty as dependence and poverty as lack of freedom—are useful in illuminating the causes and cures of poverty. They stress social and economic relationships, in contrast to definitions of poverty which stress income.

The usual discussion of poverty is in terms of an income taxonomy. The typical study shows that those who earn less than some "poverty" income level ($3,720 in 1970 for a family of four) have certain characteristics. Generally, the poor people are over sixty-five, or children, or mothers heading families, or the uneducated, or members of minority groups.[1] Low income is explained in terms of the nature of the relationship, or the lack of connection, with the labor market. The traditional framework of wage theory has in recent years been augmented by work in human-capital theory and by efforts to incorporate into traditional price theory concepts individual preferences for segregation.[2] Such an approach, while in many ways useful, must be supplemented by an understanding of the history of ideas behind the nature of a person's claim to societal resources. The evolving concepts of social as opposed to strictly market allocations must also be understood. One important distinction is whether an individual has a firm attachment to the labor market or, in the absence of such participation, is totally dependent upon unilateral government transfers. A related issue is the nature and extent of societal responsibility for those who are dependent upon such transfers.

The Poverty Line

When politicians talk about eliminating poverty, they are usually referring to the elevation of family incomes above the arbitrarily determined poverty line ($3,531 in 1968 as compared to a median

[1] See Alan B. Batchelder, *The Economics of Poverty* (New York: John Wiley and Sons, 1966), chapter 2; and Mollie Orshansky, "The Shape of Poverty in 1966," *Social Security Bulletin*, March 1968.
[2] Gary S. Becker, "Investments in Human Capital: A Theoretical Analysis," *Journal of Political Economy*, 1957.

family income that year of $8,632).[3] The poverty line in current use was devised by a Federal Interagency Committee using the Social Security Administration's (SSA's) poverty line. The SSA line was calculated on the assumption that poor families spent a third of their income on food. Using the Department of Agriculture's Economy Food Plan, a standardized budget "for temporary or emergency use when funds are low,"[4] means a per capita weekly food outlay of $4.90, or eighteen cents a meal. From survey data the SSA found that poor families spend about one third of their income on food. They assumed that all other family needs can be obtained for an amount equal to twice the family food requirements. The Department of Agriculture developed this special economy plan because welfare agencies refused to grant food allowances sufficient to purchase their more expensive "low-cost" diet. Only about one-fourth of the families spending at emergency levels obtain a nutritionally adequate diet.[5] Adjustments from this inadequate base are made to take account of family size, composition, age, farm or non-farm residence.

While it is useful to carefully define poverty in quantitative terms and spell out the assumptions used in the calculations made, any delineation of poverty involves a value judgment. The concept as we use it is not based on absolute minimums, but rather on government-approved norms.[6] One group of people is seen to be poor in relation to another group of people. Poor Americans have high incomes by Asian standards. The poor today enjoy higher incomes than the poor of a hundred years ago. Social, psychological, and ethical considerations inescapably influence standards. Someday, perhaps, current views will be thought of as rationalizations for an immoral distribution of wealth, and the existence of poverty

[3] *Council of Economic Advisers Annual Report* (Washington, D.C.: Government Printing Office, 1970), Table C-20, p. 200.
[4] U.S. Department of Health, Education and Welfare, *Toward A Social Report* (Washington, D.C.: Government Printing Office, 1969), p. 46.
[5] The President's Commission on Income Maintenance Programs, *Poverty Amid Plenty: The American Paradox* (Washington, D.C.: Government Printing Office, November, 1969), p. 15.
[6] See Mollie Orshansky, "How Poverty Is Measured," *Monthly Labor Review*, February 1969. The extent to which economists pursue more precise measurement can be seen in James N. Morgan and James D. Smith, "Measures of Economic Well-Offness and Their Correlates," *Papers and Proceedings of the American Economics Association*, Vol. LIX, No. 2 (May 1969).

viewed as a sign of serious malfunctioning of an economy, to be remedied above other goals.

Interpretation of not only the extent of poverty but also its causes is strongly influenced by the selection of the poverty line. Oscar Ornati has calculated

> (1) If we consider $5,000 to be the criterion of poverty, we see that much "poverty" is explained by the presence of low-paying industries. (2) If we consider $4,000 to be the criterion of poverty, we find that the different incidences of poverty in different cities are related to their differing labor-capital coefficients and to the occupational (skilled-unskilled) ratios of their industries. (3) If we consider $3,000 to be the criterion of poverty, then the different incidences of poverty among cities may be better explained by demographic composition. In this case, wage rates, labor intensivity, or occupation have little direct influence.[7]

The choice of the poverty-line cut-off has led to viewing the poor as only those who have the most tenuous relation to labor markets. The continuum presented by Ornati stresses the need to better equip individuals for competition in the labor market and to attempt to upgrade the jobs available to low-income workers. If this approach were followed, then attention would shift to the nature of available jobs and the preparation for the job markets accorded to low-income persons. (Indeed, the Manpower Development and Training Act attempts to do just that.) Poverty programs stress the $3,000 poverty line from political expediency: with limited funds, it is argued, it is better to help those most in need. Also, if funds are to be increased, the poverty line chosen "must be socially and politically credible. . . . A benchmark should neither select a group so small, in relation to all the population, that it hardly seems to deserve a general program, nor so large that a solution to the problem appears impossible."[8]

A more plausible poverty line for city dwellers is the Department of Labor's "Budget for a Moderate Living Standard," which in 1969 called for an income of $11,236 for a family of four living in

[7] Oscar A. Ornati, "Poverty in the Cities," in *Issues in Urban Economics*, ed. Harvey S. Perloff and Lowden Wingo, Jr. (Baltimore: Johns Hopkins Press, 1968), p. 351.
[8] Orshansky, "How Poverty is Measured," p. 37.

the New York Metropolitan area.[9] This budget allowed less than sixty cents a meal per person, a little over $150 a month for rent, and a little over $300 a year for family recreation. These are certainly reasonable amounts for a family living in a large urban area. The Department of Labor says this budget was designed to represent the estimated dollar cost required to maintain this family at a level of adequate living—to satisfy prevailing standards of what is necessary for health, efficiency, the nurture of children, and participation in community activities. This is not a "subsistence" budget, nor is it a "luxury" budget; it is an attempt to describe and measure a modest but adequate standard of living.[10]

The cost of such a moderate budget varies from city to city, and would be correspondingly lower in rural areas.

The preference for the SSA poverty line over the "near-poverty income line" (also developed by the SSA),[11] or the "city worker's family budget for a moderate living standard," which we have just discussed, or other similar measures is in a sense actually a political argument for greater or lesser assistance for the poor. Smaller estimates of the number of poor do not necessarily imply less commitment to the cause of greater income redistribution but often reflect merely a different tactical judgment of how best to give maximum support. Some feel that by minimizing the number of poor people we will be more willing to commit resources to the poverty program. Others think it tactically best to maximize the number of poor.

It is difficult to assess how much of contemporary concern for income redistribution is a function of past "advocate research" which has contributed greater knowledge of the problem; how much is a response to the political pressures of the liberal-labor coalition; and to what extent it is a response to black unrest and rebellion. Certainly the objective existence of widespread poverty among blacks has been increasingly recognized.

[9] Peter Kihss "Moderate Budget for Family Here Put at $11,236," *The New York Times* (January 5, 1970), p. 1.
[10] U.S. Department of Labor, Bureau of Labor Statistics, *City Worker's Family Budget* (Washington, D.C.: Government Printing Office, Autumn 1966), p. 3.
[11] Council of Economic Advisers, "Annual Report," in *Economic Report of the President*, 1969, pp. 152–153.

In 1968, 28.2 percent of nonwhite families and 45.7 percent of nonwhite unrelated individuals were poor by government standards.[12] The situation of blacks in the United States was dramatically described by President Kennedy in 1963:

> The Negro baby born in America today, regardless of the section of the nation in which he is born, has about half as much chance of completing high school as a white baby born in the same place on the same day, one-third as much chance of completing college, three times as much chance of becoming unemployed, about one-seventh as much chance of earning $10,000 a year, a life expectancy which is seven years shorter, and the prospects of earning only half as much.[13]

Another way to look at the comparative status of whites and blacks is to examine the white-black *income gap* (the difference between white and black average family incomes). In 1969, an HEW study reported, the income gap amounted to $3,790. Statistically, socio-economic status (being born of parents with low income, educational attainment, and job status) and family size accounted for $1,010 of the total amount. Job discrimination was responsible for $830 and lower educational attainment for $520. The remaining gap of $1,430 not otherwise accounted for suggests "that Negro men, relative to a group of white men of comparable family background, educational attainment, and occupational level, still receive much lower wages and salaries."[14]

Attitudes toward Poverty and Public Assistance

Granting that such differences exist is not, however, enough to stir the public to demand action, as long as most whites see the poor as unmotivated and unworthy of being given much help. Miller and

[12] U.S. Bureau of the Census, *Current Population Reports*, Series P-60, No. 68, "Poverty in the United States: 1959-1968" (Washington, D.C.: Government Printing Office, 1969), Table I, p. 11.
[13] Robert F. Kennedy, "Policies to Combat Negro Poverty," in *Goals for Urban America*, ed. Brian J. L. Berry and Jack Meltzer (Englewood Cliffs, N.J.: Prentice-Hall, 1967), p. 114. Also see U.S. Bureau of the Census, *Social and Economic Conditions of the Negroes in the United States* (Washington, D.C.: Government Printing Office, October 1967).
[14] U.S. Department of Health, Education and Welfare, *Toward a Social Report*, pp. 25–26.

Reissman have suggested that there are three main interpretations of poverty. The poor are viewed as either "undeserving," "self-defeating," or "victimized."[15]

The majority white position seems to view blacks as the "undeserving poor," seeing them as incompetent, lazy, and criminally inclined. This view stresses poverty "as a personal defect and not as a consequence of the character of the economic organization of society."[16] This attitude has been labeled the "Puritan–Horatio Alger Tradition."[17] The assumption is that each person in a society must work hard, be thrifty, and hold to a firm moral outlook, which will be rewarded with success in the economic and social spheres. Thus, "a condition of poverty is related to the lack of personal moral fiber."[18] The second outlook might be termed the "Good Samaritan–Lady Bountiful Tradition. The assumption of this tradition is that poverty is a consequence of tragic human weakness and lamentable circumstance, very possibly no fault of the victim, and that compassion is the proper attitude of the fortunate towards the less fortunate. . . ."[19] It regards personal problems and an inability to manage one's affairs successfully as the cause of the poor's failure. This approach "leads to heavy emphasis upon individual rehabilitation rather than social change as a source of improvement."[20] The author holds the third viewpoint: the poor are victims of the way the society operates. They are excluded from meaningful participation in the society, held to marginal jobs, and victimized by slumlords and ghetto merchants. Some who hold this general view place it in "the Prophet Amos–New Deal Tradition. The assumption of this tradition is that unjust conditions of society have victimized the poor and that the prosperous are often exploitative in their relationship to the poor."[21] The author goes farther than this, regarding the United States as a stratified society with an economy whose organization demands

[15] S. M. Miller and Frank Reissman, *Social Class and Social Policy* (New York: Basic Books, 1968), pp. 53–56.
[16] *Ibid.*, p. 53.
[17] Kenneth Clark and Jeannette Hopkins, *A Relevant War on Poverty* (New York: Harper & Row Torchbooks, 1970), p. 19.
[18] *Ibid.*
[19] *Ibid.*
[20] Miller and Reissman, *Social Class and Social Policy*, p. 55.
[21] Clark and Hopkins, *A Relevant War on Poverty*, p. 20.

some group at the bottom to do the less desirable work and serve as a low-cost pool of available labor to fill marginal jobs as needed. Training or rehabilitating members of this group may at times be necessary, but in general is not profitable to the private sector.

Obviously one is more sympathetic to the victims of exploitation than to people who are poor because they are too lazy to work or do not have the guts to fight and have given up trying to advance themselves. The demarcation between those who have "earned" assistance and those who have not corresponds to the division of American social welfare programs. The distinction between social insurance and public assistance is made on the basis of an existing claim or lack of a claim on society's resources based on a past relation of the individual to the labor market. Those who have contributed to the society's wealth receive more generous benefits than those who have not "earned" help. Those who have no claim through past work are punished for their impecunious state.[22]

There is a third category—the permanently disabled. It is interesting to note that people who cannot work are given more help than those judged too lazy to work. Hence the blind child qualifies for more generous treatment than dependent children under AFDC. Individuals who, it is believed, could work but will not (or at least do not) are treated harshly. In general, methods of giving assistance stabilize economic and social relationships in a way that helps the not-so-poor much more than the very poor. They lift the former out of temporary poverty, and perpetuate the poverty and dependent status of the latter. In government programs this dichotomy is maintained between the kind and magnitude of help offered those who receive payment from social insurance funds based on past contribution, and those who receive public assistance based solely on need.

Comparing Social Insurance and Public Aid

"Social insurance" programs provide, without a means test, income maintenance and other benefits as protection against loss of livelihood due to disability, loss of employment, death, ill health, and

[22] See Dorothy K. Newman, "Changing Attitudes about the Poor," *Monthly Labor Review*, February 1969.

old age. Benefits are deemed an earned right. They are based on past employment or contributions and are for the most part financed through prepayment arrangements required by law.[23]

The most prominent social insurance program is Old Age, Survivorship, and Disability Insurance (OASDI), set up under the Social Security Act of 1935, which in 1968 accounted for 66 percent of the total amount paid in government social insurance programs. In November 1969 the program was paying out $2.2 billion monthly to twenty-five million Americans.[24] Similar programs include federal railroad retirement, workmen's compensation, veterans' programs, and unemployment insurance.

These programs differ in their generosity to recipients. OASDI payments to retired workers averaged $98.86 a month as of December, 1968, and $51.21 a month to the average husband or wife of a retired worker.[25] Unemployment insurance paid at that time about 50 percent of full-time wages up to a modest maximum allowance. Excluded from such programs are the very poor, most agricultural workers and domestics, and others. Payments under social insurance programs involve little social stigma, since they are "earned" through past payments by beneficiaries.

Public aid, on the other hand, "refers to programs that provide payments in cash, kind, and services to needy individuals and families. Unlike social insurance programs, which pay benefits as an earned right, public aid programs rely on a means or income test to determine eligibility."[26] Most prominent of these, at least in the public mind, are "welfare" payments under Aid to Families with Dependent Children.

When the two types of programs are considered side by side, the government does a much better job against economic insecurity than against poverty. Those programs tied to present or past

[23] Ida C. Merriam and Alfred M. Skolnick, *Social Welfare Expenditures under Public Programs in the United States, 1926–1966*, U. S. Department of Health, Education and Welfare, Social Security Administration, No. 25 (Washington, D.C.: Government Printing Office, 1968), p. 31.
[24] Computed from U.S. Department of Health, Education and Welfare Office of Research and Statistics, Social Security Administration, *Social Security Bulletin*, March 1970, Table M-1, p. 22.
[25] *Ibid.*, Table M-12, p. 30.
[26] Merriam and Skolnick, *Social Welfare Expenditures under Public Programs in the United States, 1929–1966*, p. 73.

labor-market roles prove more generous in their benefits, on the whole, than public assistance. The comparison is made more difficult by the manner in which programs are administered. For example, the program that gets most attention, Aid to Families with Dependent Children, is administered by the states, who set payment benefits. In May 1968, payments per recipient ranged from $8.45 a month in Mississippi to $68.55 in New York, with a national average of $40.95.

Dividing social welfare expenditures for 1968 into social insurance, public aid, and veterans' benefits yields the figures in Table 5.1.

Table 5.1   Social Welfare Expenditures by Major Programs in 1968

PROGRAM	EXPENDITURES IN MILLIONS OF DOLLARS
Social insurance	$37,866.9
Public Assistance	5,671.9
Veterans' payments	4,616.0

Computed from: U.S. Department of Health, Education and Welfare, Office of Research and Statistics, Social Security Administration, *Social Security Bulletin*, March 1970, Table M-1, p. 22.

In addition, other expenditures should be included if we are concerned with social welfare—housing, education, and so on. All types of federal aid to the poor by major category are shown in Table 5.2.

In recent years about 12 percent of GNP has been spent on social welfare. Public aid (what is commonly termed "welfare") amounts to about one percent of GNP. To get an idea of the relative magnitude of the various programs, one must consider the expenditures presented in Table 5.3. In December of 1968 there were 2.8 million persons receiving Old Age Assistance, Aid to the Blind, or Aid to the Permanently and Totally Disabled, at an annual cost of $2.6 billion. There were at the same time 1.5 million families with 6.1 million individual members who received $2.8 billion from AFDC. One would imagine that few Americans would be able to guess that these were the relative magnitudes involved. The hue and cry over "welfare" payments to reward mothers for having so many children hardly corresponds to the importance of this item in the total budget.

Table 5.2 Federal Aid to the Poor

	ACTUAL 1969	ESTIMATED 1970	ESTIMATED 1971
	IN BILLIONS	IN BILLIONS	IN BILLIONS
Education	$ 2.2	$ 2.3	$ 2.7
Employment assistance	1.6	1.7	2.3
Health assistance	5.3	5.9	6.4
Maintenance of individuals and families			
Income assistance	15.1	17.1	17.8
Other Maintenance assistance	1.6	2.3	3.3
Research, demonstrations and			
other support	0.4	0.4	0.4
Total	$26.2	$29.7	$32.9

Source: Special Analyses: Budget of the United States FY 1971 (Washington, D.C.: Government Printing Office, 1970), p. 192; reprinted in American Enterprise Institute for Public Policy Research, *The Bill to Revamp the Welfare System* (Washington, D.C.: American Enterprise Institute for Public Policy Research, 1970).

Table 5.3 Selected Welfare Expenditures in 1968

PROGRAM	EXPENDITURES IN MILLIONS OF DOLLARS
Unemployment benefits (including Railroad unemployment benefits)	$ 2,327.7
Workmen's compensation	1,525.0
Aid to Families with Dependent Children	2,823.8
Old Age, Survivorship, and Disability Insurance	24,936.5

Source: U.S. Department of Health, Education and Welfare, Office of Research and Statistics, Social Security Administration, *Social Security Bulletin*, March 1970, Table M-1, p. 22, and Table M-24, p. 41.

Social Security actually provides more cash income to the poor than do all other programs of public assistance. This occurs because there is a strong bias in government welfare programs, in terms of absolute expenditures, toward helping the aged as a group, and many of the aged are poor. As Henry J. Aaron has shown, "Roughly two-thirds of cash transfers to the poor go to the aged, who in 1966 were 18 percent of the poor."[27]

"In 1965, only 20 percent of poor persons received public assistance payments and, of these, 82 percent remained poor after payment."[28] Public assistance did not really begin to help the poor. Considering all forms of transfer payments, again for 1965, the Census Bureau found, "Only two-thirds of all households that would be poor with no public payments receive any help. Of these poor as we now count them—after all payments—fully half have received no help at all from a public income program. Of those who do receive public assistance, 5 out of 6 remain poor after they get assistance. By contrast, social security, less restrictive in other income that beneficiaries may have, lifts more than half the household poor without their payments into the nonpoor ranks."[29]

Evaluating Programs to Help the Poor

What do all these statistics tell us? First, that income maintenance programs are more successful in achieving their goals than public assistance programs. Second, that many of the poor receive little or no assistance from government.[30] In spite of these statistics, pressure has mounted in the general public and in Congress to stop what appears to be a rapid increase in the number of welfare recip-

[27] Henry J. Aaron, "Income Transfer Programs," *Monthly Labor Review*, February 1969, p. 53.
[28] U.S. Department of Health, Education and Welfare, *Toward a Social Report*, p. 49.
[29] Orshansky, "How Poverty Is Measured," p. 41.
[30] Orshansky, "The Shape of Poverty in 1966"; U.S. Department of Health, Education and Welfare, Advisory Council on Public Welfare. *Having the Power, We Have the Duty* (Washington, D.C.: Government Printing Office, June 1966); Aaron, "Income Transfer Programs" and Elizabeth Herzog, "Facts and Fictions about the Poor," *Monthly Labor Review*, February 1969.

ients, especially AFDC cases. The period from 1953 to the beginning of 1967 witnessed a 407-percent increase in the number of children for whom AFDC payments were made.

In 1967 Congress passed what Daniel P. Moynihan has called "the first purposively punitive welfare legislation in the history of the American national government,"[31] a bill which restricted further increases in the number of welfare recipients. "Inasmuch as no effort was made to conceal the fact that these provisions were designed to halt the rise in *Negro* dependence on the AFDC program," Moynihan adds, "the House action might also be considered the first deliberate anti-civil rights measure of the present era."[32]

The increase in the number of program recipients under AFDC could be stemmed, Congress believed, through more stringent efforts to encourage mothers to work and by putting ceilings on spending. It is hard to see how a mother with children, living on AFDC payments of $40.95 a month per person, could prefer receiving welfare to working if there were day-care centers and decently paying jobs available to her. Congress, not concerned with the testimony of sociologists (many still confused sociology with socialism), was out to punish "rioters" and "freeloaders."

In April 1967, *The New York Times* featured a report of a special White House study in a column one, page one story headed: "U.S. Finds Only 1% on Welfare Lists Are Able to Work."[33] At the same time economists were finding evidence that "welfare payments under the program of Aid to Families with Dependent Children deter parents from seeking work."[34] Studies have also shown that when jobs are scarce, AFDC rates will *ceteris paribus* rise.[35]

[31] Daniel P. Moynihan, "Crisis in Welfare," *The Public Interest*, Winter 1968, p. 3.

[32] *Ibid.*

[33] *The New York Times*, April 20, 1967, p. 1.

[34] Herschel Kasper, "Welfare Payments and Work Incentives: Some Determinants of the Rates of General Assistance Payments," *Journal of Human Resources*, Winter 1968, p. 88.

[35] Daniel R. Fusfeld, "The Basic Economics of the Urban and Racial Crisis," in *Conference Papers of the Union for Radical Political Economics* (Ann Arbor, Mich.: The Union for Radical Political Economics, 1968), p. 71, citing a study by Marjorie Hanson, "The Effects of Welfare Payments on Labor Force Participation: Preliminary Findings" (mimeo, 1968).

Even when jobs are available, welfare discourages people from working. As Brehm and Savings have shown, significant numbers of potential workers have been discouraged from seeking work because of what has amounted to a 100-percent tax.[36] For every dollar earned, assistance payments were lowered. In 1968 this "tax" was lowered to only 70 percent with a $30 exemption; the very poor pay the same marginal tax rate as those with $200,000 or more in income. (Of course, this high-income group had an *effective* tax rate of close to 30 percent, while the person giving up assistance paid a full 70 percent tax.) There is a problem of disincentives when tax rates for working are so high and potential earnings so low.

The American attitudes traditionally shown toward the poor can be summarized as voluntarism, localism, and paternalism. The American belief that local communities are the essential foundation of democracy and that governmental functions are best carried out at the local level established the domination of the local elite-controlled charity approach to helping the poor. The Christmas basket, which proved the innate goodness of the giver and the expectation that the humble poor would do their part by showing proper gratitude to their betters, has died slowly. The voluntary agencies were, in fact, often an important force in resisting more advanced welfare concepts. "It will be recalled," Morris and Rein remind us, "that the Charity Organization Society bitterly opposed public pension schemes for widows and children lest such programs might come to be regarded as a right."[37]

The interpretation of public assistance as a gift rather than a right also guides congressional action, the 1967 legislation being the most blatant manifestation of this attitude. When this interpretation has been combined with the desire to cut down on government expenditures, even the minimal protections allowed

---

[36] C. T. Brehm and T. R. Savings, "The Demand for General Assistance Payments," *American Economic Review*, December 1964, p. 1017. Also see Bruno Stein and Peter S. Albin, "The Demand for General Assistance Payments: Comment," *American Economic Review*, June 1967; and C. T. Brehm and T. R. Savings, "Reply," *American Economic Review*, June 1967.
[37] Robert Morris and Martin Rein, "Emerging Patterns in Community Planning," in *Urban Planning and Social Policy*, ed. B. J. Frieden and Robert Morris (New York: Basic Books, 1968), p. 23.

welfare recipients have often been ignored. One writer, commenting on Senate Appropriations Committee hearings, has said: "From the constitutional viewpoint, the equitable treatment of applicants and recipients is at least as important, if not far more so, than saving tax funds. . . . But no effort was expended to learn if constitutional rights had been denied vulnerable poor families, as experts knew was happening."[38]

There are two ways of viewing welfare administration. First it can be argued that what is needed is to convince men of good will that the poor do have rights which should be protected, that the American welfare system should live up to its responsibility to the poor. A second viewpoint entails seeing the welfare system as actually carrying out only too well its function—a function of colonial administration. This second approach perceives the function of welfare agencies to be the policing of the poor. "Strongly put, the main impact of many social-welfare programs has been to provide enough services to keep the 'natives' from becoming too distressed. The aim has been to 'cool out' their anger rather than to help them out of poverty."[39]

Typically, the economic aid which is given, whether by welfare workers or by public housing personnel, is patterned on the donee's "unquestioning acceptance of an expert's dictation of what is 'good for the client,' and of an administrator's unchecked and unreviewable authority to terminate assistance."[40]

This pattern has a number of serious consequences. First, the donee is dependent upon the agency staff worker. His role is passive. He is administered to. This is not a relationship which breeds self-confidence. Second, since the client has no real power to influence the agency, the agency feels no pressure to perform more efficiently. The consumer is forced to accept the product. Third, there is a tendency for the agency to avoid risks which would jeopardize its appropriations, or for the individual staff member, his job. Fourth, there is a tendency for the agency to treat all cases alike and not to depart from this uniform treatment, no matter

[38] Winifred Bell, "The Rights of the Poor: Welfare Witch-hunts in the District of Columbia," *Social Work*, January 1968, p. 67.
[39] Morris and Rein, "Emerging Patterns in Community Planning," p. 197.
[40] Edgar S. Cahn and Jean C. Cahn, "The War on Poverty: A Civilian Perspective," *Yale Law Journal*, July 1964, pp. 1321–1322.

how worthy such an exception may seem. Rules in a centrally directed agency cannot be flexible. Further, differences between the lower-level staff and the executive staff are resolved by the latter, who may lack real contact with ongoing operations. Fifth, agencies are responsive to pressure, not from their clients but from political authorities. Sixth, since funding is based on past success, there is pressure on the agency to produce dramatic results. This may lead the agency to inflate its "success ratio" by taking the easier cases, as, for example, has been done in some job retraining programs. Seventh, the behavior of agency staff members cannot be fully regulated by the laws governing the organization. The existence of alleged technicalities of law or the alleged statutory inability of an official to redress a grievance is often correlated with who is presenting the grievance and how it is being presented. The extent to which the rich are able to threaten legal action and the poor are not may influence the disposition of any individual case being handled by a bureaucracy. This matter of legal rights is another face of the inequality of opportunity for the poor. Radical lawyers defending the poor, their salaries often paid by the government, and recent court decisions have helped, but the problem of inequality before the law remains.

Welfare colonialism is created, then, not only by the way the wider society treats the poor, and especially the nonwhite poor, but also by the relationship between professional social workers and the poor which lends itself so easily to paternalism. As Preston Wilcox has suggested, "Social agencies need helpless people in order to have people to help. Added to that is the fact that even the most open-minded people can't accept the poor even as potential equals. The result is that some workers, quite unconsciously, see their job as a sedative for social ills rather than a good hard push toward change."[41] It is hard to see how the social worker in his conventional role could offer "a good hard push for change." The kind of help he can offer is too limited to do much. He can offer no long-run solution. He can only help reduce, and only slightly reduce, the physical deprivation, to help the poor "adjust to their condition," and help them think more "positively" about

---

[41] Cited in Patricia Cayo Sexton, *Spanish Harlem: Anatomy of Poverty* (New York: Harper Colophon Books, 1965), p. 100.

their condition. "The usual social work methods are as effective in combating mass poverty as a spear is in knocking out armored tanks."[42] If the social worker can be criticized for not helping the poor organize themselves to demand changes in the welfare system's paternalism, perhaps it is fair also to ask whether society would approve such an emphasis. Most Americans would not. Marris and Rein point out, this may take place without collusion or conscious recognition of self-interest. Still, "the values, tastes, and distastes of middle-class America naturally conspire to render as little to the less fortunate as its own security and conscience will allow."[43] Certainly the middle class is hesitant to be more heavily taxed to help the poor attain standards that would threaten their own status. Better schools for the poor and open admissions to college mean more competition and fewer resources for their children, and a threat to the privileged advancement of their children. While many of the paternal aspects of the present system might be overcome through direct assistance (as in a negative income tax, or Nixon's Family Assistance Plan, which will be discussed below), most of the suggestions for changing the welfare program do little to bring about greater equality of opportunity.

Changing the American Welfare System

If poverty is best viewed as dependence, and if the role of public assistance is to perpetuate dependence—a treatment of the poor to which most middle-class Americans give their implicit assent— what fundamental change is needed in the welfare system, and how can it be brought about?

There are three types of change in our social welfare system which compete for attention: (1) increase the efficiency of operation and level of payments under the present system, (2) modify it to give more individualized attention to client needs with programs of rehabilitation, and (3) change the institutions which work to create dependence.

[42] *Ibid.*, p. 168.
[43] Peter Marris and Martin Rein, *Dilemmas of Social Reform: Poverty and Community Action in the United States* (New York: Atherton Press, 1967), p. 45.

The first approach accepts the caretaker function as the dominant focus of welfare. The kinds of changes it espouses in the present system are national standards for welfare eligibility and payments based on uniform schedules. Such a reform would be useful; the economic problems of one part of the country (the rural South, for example) may certainly have the effect of increasing welfare payments elsewhere (the North, for instance). Migration places heavier burdens on some areas (especially the central cities) than others (the suburbs). The assumption of total financial responsibility for welfare payments by the national government can also be supported on the grounds that children should not have to suffer because of their parents' income status (40 percent of the poor are children), nor should welfare recipients in low-income states live on the verge of starvation because their state legislatures are unable or unwilling to offer them substantial assistance. The Nixon administration moved in this direction through recognition that "poverty is a national problem which happens to be geographically concentrated" and "federal administration would reduce the difficulties arising from major differences in local standards of benefits, eligibility, and administration."[44] The major contribution in this area by the Nixon administration is the acceptance of the minimum-income concept. By providing a family of four which has no other earnings with $1600 and allowing it to keep the first $720 of earnings and fifty cents of each dollar after that, the initial Nixon proposal succeeded in offering some minimal income to all families without discouraging work or encouraging the breakup of families. This was to be accomplished under a system which could be administered impersonally without social worker-investigators or bureaucratic red tape.

While the plan extended aid to six million families not previously covered under public assistance programs, payments to each family were very modest—less than half the government's own conservative poverty line. Most states, in fact, already were giving benefits greater than those proposed under the plan. The legislation also required that these states provide supplementary benefits so that those already receiving benefits would not be worse off

[44] Council of Economic Advisers, "Annual Report," in *Economic Report of the President*, 1969, p. 166.

under the new program. The Nixon plan was an improvement over existing benefits in only twenty states, mostly in the South.

Alice Rivlin, a former official of the Department of Health, Education and Welfare and an expert on income maintenance programs, suggests that "The fact that the plan does not go far enough does not make it less worthy of enthusiastic support as a first step."[45] The writer is not so sure. In fact, the Nixon Administration may have, through this relatively inexpensive program, taken the pressure off for more far-reaching changes. Further, the Nixon plan does not really change the status quo very much. Power relations are left intact. The low-income population is helped only to a limited degree. Confrontation is avoided, and a growing welfare-rights group finds some of its liberal supporters satisfied that ample progress is being made. Most importantly the program fails to provide access for the poor into productive participation in the economy. The provisions that require able-bodied persons to work or accept job training where available as a condition for aid (except in the case of mothers with pre-school children) leaves room for the exploitation of the poor at low-wage, dead-end jobs. The threat of withdrawal of aid, especially since it can be exercised by state and local agencies guided by local prejudice, creates the potential for extreme abuse. *The New York Times* may be right in calling the new welfare plan "the most fundamental welfare reform in nearly four decades," but from the viewpoint of ending poverty, it is a very small step.[46] The work requirements, combined with the local control over decentralized manpower programs, open the door to regressive effects.

There are other changes in existing programs which could be considered. Renewed effort could be placed on taking welfare goals under existing law and defining them more completely in operational terms, by deciding what needs people have (health, housing, etc.) and how many people lacking a stipulated list of goods and services are eligible for them; and then by reaching out to this "client population" to see that they are served. Agency performance would thus be based on how closely its clientele corre-

---

[45] Alice M. Rivlin, "Nixon's Welfare Reform: Good But Not Enough," *The Progressive*, October 1969.
[46] Editorial, *The New York Times*, March 8, 1970.

sponds to its client population, and whether clients are served according to acceptable standards.[47]

A second approach is to focus on rehabilitation rather than "protective caretaking." The whole complex of legislation described under the rubric of manpower development takes this approach, seeking to help those who are able-bodied but whose lack of general education and job skills consigns them to a marginal position in the economy.[48] Charles Killingsworth argues that income supplements without such remedial services are not enough. "A transfer payment system is likely to leave untouched the root causes of poverty. At best, such a system will maintain its clients at a level a dollar a year above the poverty line. The transfer payment improves the buying power of the poor; remedial services seek to improve the earning power of the poor."[49] This approach is discussed at length in the next chapter where the labor market is considered.

The third approach, demanding structural reform of institutions which create dependency, has been advocated by recipients and social workers alike. John B. Turner, addressing an audience of social workers in 1968, urged the profession to adopt this stance.

> The concepts of caretaking and rehabilitation are too limited in definition, as it becomes clearer that it is not just people who are deprived, ill, and unskilled, but that our communities, our social, economic, and political structures are also sick, dys-functional, deprived, in need of crisis intervention, and in need of rehabilitation. If social work is to be more responsive to the human crisis it must operate from a concept sufficiently broad to embrace the range of front-line institutional functions that are required to produce and to maintain a socially productive man in a humanized society.[50]

[47] See Janet S. Reiner, Everett Reiner, and Thomas A. Reiner, "Client Analysis and the Planning of Public Programs," in Frieden and Morris, *Urban Planning and Social Policy.*
[48] See U.S. Department of Labor, *A Report on Manpower Requirements, Resources, Utilization, and Training* (Washington, D.C.: Government Printing Office, annually).
[49] Charles Killingsworth, *Jobs and Income for Negroes* (Ann Arbor, Mich.: Institute of Labor and Industrial Relations, University of Michigan, 1968), p. 81.
[50] John B. Turner, "In Response to Change, Social Work at the Crossroads," *Social Work,* July 1968, p. 9.

One of the most influential voices calling for change in social welfare practices is Richard Titmuss. Titmuss's analysis starts with questioning the premises upon which welfare payments are given. He thinks that the view of the average citizen who "sees public welfare expenditure—particularly expenditure which is redistributive in intent—as a burden, an impediment to growth and economic development,"[51] is mistaken. As the rationale is mistaken, so is the program which follows from it. Government welfare programs which are kept to a minimum to avoid "waste" are misguided in Titmuss's view because there is a complementary relation between welfare and national efficiency.[52] A productive person contributes to economic growth and therefore a welfare program aimed at prevention and rehabilitation by increasing a person's ability to hold a job adds to GNP. Furthermore, in an "unequal and class-saturated society," urban blight and slum living, obsolescence of skills, the poor preparation some public school systems give, and the influence of segregation and discrimination all generate "diswelfares." "If," suggests Titmuss, "identification of the agents of diswelfare were possible—if we could legally name and blame the culprits—then, in theory at least, redress could be obtained through the courts by the method of monetary compensation for damages. But multiple causalities and the diffusion of disservices—the modern cholera of change—make this solution impossible. We have, therefore, as societies to make other choices; either to provide social services, or to allow the social costs of the system to lie where they fall."[53] For many recipients of welfare services the benefits they receive "represent partial compensations for disservices."[54] When southern sharecroppers are forced off the land by technological advances in agriculture, when coal miners must move on because of mechanization, and when these people come to cities where they are unable to find work, how should they be treated? "Can we and should we, in providing benefits and compensation . . . distinguish between 'faults' in the individual (moral, psychological, or social) and the

[51] Richard M. Titmuss, *Commitment to Welfare* (New York: Pantheon, 1968), pp. 124–125.
[52] *Ibid.*, p. 130.
[53] *Ibid.*, p. 133.
[54] *Ibid.*

'faults of society'?"[55] When the Congress waits too long to pass needed fiscal policy legislation and unemployment stays unnecessarily high, is it the fault of the jobless that they cannot find work?

When Titmuss's approach to the problems of the urban ghetto is applied to the "victimized poor," they are not merely seen as deserving of generosity in the form of charity; they have a claim on society—a debt is owed. Lawrence Haworth makes the point forcefully.

> . . . [T]he poor are not merely beneficiaries but they are a group who, as a group, are *wronged*, and in attempting to improve their condition we are undertaking to right the wrong. This circumstance makes the term "beneficiary" somewhat misleading. In any strict sense, if injustice is at issue, a poverty program is not something we do "for the poor"—as if morally we could enact it or not as we chose and as if we were morally indifferent whether we do so or not—but the poor *exact* the program, they demand it as a matter of right. There is no charity in it, any more so than there is charity in repaying a debt or paying properly exacted damages.[56]

This view is held by very few white Americans. Most can be divided into those who would give somewhat more to the poor, and some who wish to give less. If less assistance is given, conditions worsen, tensions rise. Marginal increases, while they may be well publicized, are often rightly characterized as tokenism.

There may in fact be a "rat hole effect" at work, in which piecemeal programs do little to break dependency patterns, and funds are soon dissipated on salaries for agency workers and minimal consumption allowances for the poor. Since the funds spent are spread too thinly to successfully overcome the forces of downward cumulative causation, they do not really help. The funds are "wasted," the situation is not improved, and conservatives call for lower expenditures.

Sometimes programs do succeed in helping individuals, but since funds are limited, the number helped is usually not very great. As the lagging anti-poverty crusade goes into its second decade of

[55] *Ibid.*, p. 134.
[56] Lawrence Haworth, "Deprivation and the Good City," in *Power, Poverty, and Urban Policy*, ed. Warner Bloomberg, Jr., and Henry J. Schmandt (Beverly Hills, Calif.: Sage Publications, 1968), p. 40.

operation, surely the use of the term "demonstration program" must bring embarrassment to agency heads. When demonstrations succeed they are never expanded on the necessary broad base. Instead, new "demonstrations" take place.

The tragedy of the social welfare program is in a sense only part of the larger society's tragedy. Allocation of resources through the price system means that the defeated in the economic struggle—the aged, the families headed by women, and the minority groups—are seen as inferior human beings, as losers. The fact is that the game demands that someone lose, and the deck is stacked against those least able to do anything about it. Dependence is perpetuated over years and generations.

The most vociferous deniers of the debt owed the poor are the people only a few steps higher up the pyramid. Those who have something, even if it is very little, want to protect what is theirs against those who have still less. The connection between these two groups is crucial in determining the outcome of the current pull between right and left in this country. It will be resolved for better or for worse in terms of the struggle between a dying individualism which masks corporate greed and an as-yet-unformed concept of societal responsibility. The job market which preserves the individual nature of the struggle for economic resources and acts as the allocating mechanism is one crucial area in which new patterns of social organization will emerge. In the next chapter, we shall examine the labor market and its treatment of the low-income, and especially the black, worker.

CHAPTER 6

The Ghetto Worker
and the Labor Market

A man's occupation is probably the most important fact we can know about him. With that information, we can say a great deal about where he lives, how he lives, and where he fits into the social system. Low social status usually excludes a person or a group from the better occupational choices a society has to offer. Thus we find blacks in low-paying, low-status positions.[1] In this chapter we are concerned with the mechanisms through which blacks are denied meaningful participation in job markets, and with exploring avenues for ending their exclusion.

Some scholars have suggested that "the central fact about the American underclass is that it is created by the operation of what in other ways is the most successful economic system known to man. It is not, in short, so much that the good system has not included the underclass, as that the manner of its operation produces and reproduces it."[2]

---

[1] The evidence is presented in Ray Marshall, *The Negro Worker* (New York: Random House, 1967); and Arthur M. Ross and Herbert Hill, eds., *Employment, Race, and Poverty* (New York: Harcourt, Brace and World, 1967).
[2] Lee Rainwater, "Looking Back and Looking Up," *Trans-Action*, February 1969, p. 9.

Other students stress that the historical trend of growth in GNP has diminished the extent of poverty, suggesting that adding to the amount of capital per worker and investing more in his education, training, and health will continue to bring about gradual progress. "The soundest and surest way to reduce poverty year after year is to improve the potential productivity of all persons, including the poor."[3]

Both of these views are correct. Where one chooses to place emphasis depends upon the degree to which one identifies with the immediate needs of the American underclass, and upon how serious one believes the social costs of our present pattern of growth to be. It also depends upon whether one acknowledges that racism has played an integral part in American economic development, that plantation slaves and ghetto blacks have been a crucial source of capital accumulation, and that the fruits of their labors have been appropriated by whites. We have argued the validity of these assertions. That blacks have received some of the fruits of their labor is not to be doubted. Unquestionably black real incomes have risen—but the exploitative nature of black-white relations has not changed.

Our concern here is with the nature and availability of jobs and with wages paid in ghetto labor markets. Black workers, even when they are able to find jobs, are generally poorly paid. The economy provides work for the black underclass, but not the chance for advancement. The labor market, in fact, functions to maintain blacks in the role of exploited undifferentiated labor. Most blacks are allowed only a marginal attachment to the labor force, as we shall show.

At the outset it is useful to try to gain some perspective on the problem in three ways: first, by a quick look at some income and employment data; second, by a consideration of how employers and other whites on the one hand, and ghetto blacks on the other, view the level of unemployment and the seriousness of discrimination in the job market; third, by an evaluation of the usefulness of human capital theory, dealt with briefly in the last chapter. After

[3] Robert J. Lampman, "Prognosis for Poverty," in National Tax Association, *Proceedings of the Fifty-Seventh Annual Conference*, ed. Walter J. Kress (Harrisburg, Pa.: National Tax Association, 1964), p. 74.

these preliminaries we shall examine the workings of the labor market and the extent to which it systematically discriminates against blacks. We shall consider its functioning in terms of two competing concepts of the labor market: queuing and dual markets. Finally, we shall deal with programs to assist black workers.

The Unemployment Experience of Black Workers

In 1960 the white unemployment rate was 4.9 percent, while the nonwhite rate was 10.2 percent. In the prosperous years that followed, the unemployment rates fell. In 1969 white unemployment was 3.1 percent, while nonwhite was 6.4 percent. Blacks have experienced over twice the incidence of unemployment of whites. The ratio of nonwhite to white unemployment remained almost constant.[4] By the spring of 1970, unemployment rates had risen to close to five percent, threatening to go still higher, bringing a cancellation of job-training contracts by major manufacturing firms and the laying off of many hard-core unemployed who had been hired during a period of labor shortage. "Real" unemployment for blacks was much worse than these statistics indicate, because one effect of discrimination is to force blacks to take jobs below their skill levels and to limit many to involuntary part-time employment. A useful concept in approximating "real" unemployment is the *subemployment rate*. Subemployment is officially defined as the sum of (1) unemployed persons, (2) part-time workers seeking full-time work, (3) full-time workers who are heads of households and earn less than $3,120 per year ($2,800 per year if not a head of household), (4) 50 percent of the adult males not in the labor force, and (5) 50 percent of the estimated "unfound" adult

[4] *Annual Report of the Council of Economic Advisers*, Table C-24 (Washington, D.C.: Government Printing Office, 1970), p. 205. Also see U.S. Department of Labor, Bureau of Labor Statistics; and U.S. Department of Commerce, Bureau of the Census, *Social and Economic Conditions of Negroes in the United States*, (Washington, D.C.: Government Printing Office); and U.S. Bureau of the Census, *Current Population Reports*, Series P-23, Special Studies (formerly Technical Studies), No. 27, "Trends in Social and Economic Conditions in Metropolitan Areas" (Washington, D.C.: Government Printing Office, 1969).

males.[5] In this last classification are persons who cannot be traced by investigators. Census figures probably underestimate still further because of fear on the part of the interviewees. For example, Patricia Cayo Sexton reports on a house-to-house canvass by trusted neighbors in the triangle area of Spanish Harlem which in 1961 found 10,000 persons where the 1960 census listed 6,100.[6] In defining subemployment as it has, the Department of Labor believes it has used a "very conservative measure."[7]

While unemployment in the Standard Metropolitan Statistical Area (SMSA) of New York was 4.6 percent in 1966, unemployment in Central Harlem was 8.1 percent, and subemployment was 29 percent. On St. Louis's North Side, subemployment was 39 percent, compared with an SMSA unemployment rate of 4.5 percent. So again, the magnitude of the problem was greater for the ghetto dweller than for the non-ghetto dweller. Over-all, the 1966 special study of ten slum areas by the Department of Labor found that "one out of every three slum residents who were already workers, or should and could become workers with suitable help, was either jobless or earning only substandard wages."[8] In 1966 subemployment for nonwhite men as a group was 22 percent compared to 8 percent for white men.[9] Black median family income in 1967 was 62 percent of white family income. Blacks both earned less than whites and were unemployed and underemployed more.

Subjective Evaluations of Black Labor Force Experience

It would seem logical that subjective judgments of the severity of the unemployment problem would reflect the experience of those

[5] See U.S. Department of Labor, *A Report on Manpower Requirements, Resources, Utilization, and Training* (Washington, D.C.: Government Printing Office, 1968), pp. 34–35. A reader interested in how employment is measured should see U.S. Bureau of Labor Statistics, *How the Government Measures Unemployment*, Report No. 312 (Washington, D.C.: Government Printing Office, June 1967).
[6] Patricia Cayo Sexton, *Spanish Harlem: Anatomy of Poverty* (New York: Harper Colophon Books, 1966), p. 87.
[7] U.S. Department of Labor, *A Report on Manpower Requirements, Resources, Utilization, and Training*, p. 34.
[8] *Ibid.*, p. 34.
[9] *Ibid.*, p. 35.

who make such judgments. The results of two surveys of attitudes towards discrimination in the job market bear this out.

At the request of the Kerner Commission a group of Johns Hopkins social scientists interviewed the managers and personnel officers of the largest employer institutions in fifteen large northern cities. The firms were selected because it was felt they represented "the most economically progressive institutions in America."[10] The findings revealed that while the businessmen on the whole did not show openly racist attitudes, their feelings could be termed "gentlemanly white racism" as "evident in a tacit, but often unwitting, acceptance of institutional practices that subordinate or exclude Negroes."[11] When these men were asked if they thought unemployment was a very serious problem in the nation's cities, only 21 percent thought it was, compared to 26 percent who thought air pollution and 31 percent who thought traffic to be "very serious."[12] *From their point of view,* air pollution and traffic affect them, and so *are* more serious problems than unemployment, which they do not experience.

In their hiring practices these men followed standards which were not openly racist but which had the effect of excluding ghetto workers from consideration. The criteria they used in hiring were (a) previous experience of the applicant and (b) recommendations. These criteria are good from the business point of view, but ghetto blacks are unlikely to have had strong previous labor force experience, and few of them know persons who could write recommendations for them. They are not likely to be viewed as "qualified" for available jobs. From the employer's point of view, he is merely avoiding bad risks. If the black lacks adequate qualifications for the job, in the typical businessman's view, this is to be blamed on historical or environmental causes. Of the "progressive" firms interviewed, there was a median black representation of one percent in professional positions and two percent in skilled jobs,

[10] See Peter H. Rossi, Richard A. Berk, David P. Boesel, Bettye K. Eidson, and W. Eugene Groves, "Between White and Black: The Facts of American Institutions in the Ghetto," *Supplemental Studies for the National Advisory Commission on Civil Disorders* (Washington, D.C.: Government Printing Office, July 1968).
[11] David Boesel, Richard Berk, W. Eugene Groves, Bettye Eidson, and Peter H. Rossi, "White Institutions and Black Rage," *Trans-Action,* March 1969, p. 25.
[12] *Ibid.*

while 20 percent were black in the unskilled job classification.[13] Even as the businessman perpetuates black exclusion, he can claim individual innocence. It is not his fault, nor the blacks', but "the system's."

In another study of the same fifteen cities, blacks were asked whether they believed that "some or many blacks had been turned down for jobs because of race." Seventy-one percent said, "Yes," they did. Thirty percent responded that they personally had been refused jobs because of racial prejudice. Sixty-eight percent thought that "some or many blacks missed out on promotions" for this reason.[14] In response to the announced breakthroughs in hiring practices, it is interesting to note that 77 percent believed that "big companies hire a few Negroes only for show purposes, to appear to be non-discriminatory."[15] Blacks and whites looking at the same situation perceive it very differently. This leads whites to underestimate seriously the degree to which blacks feel oppressed.

The importance of attitudes towards employment opportunities in shaping a person's sense of personal worth is hard to state strongly enough. Two black psychiatrists interpreting from their experience in public and private practice suggest that:

> As boys approach adulthood, masculinity becomes more and more bound up with money making. In a capitalistic society economic wealth is inextricably interwoven with manhood. Closely allied is power—power to control and direct other men, power to influence the course of one's own and other lives. The more lives one can influence, the greater the power. The ultimate power is the freedom to understand and alter one's life. It is this power, both individually and collectively, which has been denied the black man.[16]

The Importance of a Tight Labor Market

Just as individual experience conditions personal attitudes, so the sum of these attitudes is embodied in a national policy consensus.

[13] *Ibid.*
[14] Angus Campbell and Howard Schuman, "Racial Attitudes in Fifteen American Cities," *Supplemental Studies for the National Advisory Commission on Civil Disorders* (Washington, D.C.: Government Printing Office, July 1968), p. 23.
[15] *Ibid.*
[16] Grier and Cobbs, *Black Rage*, p. 50.

Consider the relation between unemployment and inflation. Economists find that, historically, high rates of inflation accompany full employment and that as unemployment increases, inflation decreases—the so-called Phillips curve relationship.[17] Given the structure of the American economy, getting more people employed puts a strain on the system because it is accompanied by inflation. Whether the nation accepts more inflation or more unemployment is, of course, a political judgment. In the post-Korea, pre-Vietnam years the country accepted high rates of unemployment to preserve price stability. A very low rate of unemployment has resulted, for the most part, only in time of war. It is not a coincidence that it has been in just such periods that the gains of nonwhite workers have been most impressive. In arguing that a low rate of unemployment may be the single most important policy variable in aiding the nonwhite worker, James Tobin explains:

> In a tight labor market unemployment is low and short in duration, and job vacancies are plentiful. People who stand at the end of the hiring line and the top of the layoff list have the most to gain from a tight labor market. It is not surprising that the position of Negroes relative to that of whites improves in a tight labor market and declines in a slack market.[18]
>
> In a slack labor market, employers can pick and choose, both in recruiting and in promoting. They exaggerate the skill, education, and experience requirements of their jobs. They use diplomas, or color, or personal histories as convenient screening devices. In a tight market, they are forced to be realistic, to tailor job specifications to the available supply, and to give on-the-job training.[19]

A question which should be explored is why this inflation-employment trade-off is so much worse in the United States than in countries like Sweden, Germany, or Japan. If it is because

[17] A. W. Phillips, "The Relation Between Unemployment and the Rate of Change of Money Wages in the United Kingdom, 1862–1952," *Economics*, November 1958; and Paul A. Samuelson and Robert M. Solow, "Problems of Achieving and Maintaining a Stable Price Level," *American Economic Review*, May 1969.
[18] James Tobin, "Improving the Economic Status of the Negro," in *The American Negro*, ed. Talcott Parsons and Kenneth B. Clark (Boston: Beacon Press, 1967), p. 53.
[19] *Ibid.*, p. 456.

America has a monopolistic market structure insensitive to competitive pressure, then the cure is not to be found in better labor market policies. If instead (or in addition) the cause is the lack of skills of the unemployed, then training blacks and other minority groups is in everyone's interest. This second line of approach leads to the advocacy of greater expenditures on education, health facilities, and other forms of investment in "human capital."

Investment in Human Capital

Human resource study involves three interrelated areas of inquiry: first, human-capital studies which look at the inputs that increase worker productivity—formal education, on-the-job training, better nutrition, health care, and other inputs which enhance human potential. The return of such "investment" can be measured in terms of increased output per unit of input (both reduced to a common numeraire—money value). Second are the questions of equity which result from patterns of investment and factor payments (unemployment and poverty). Third are the political questions of power and social causality. The main focus of attention by economists has been on the first of these. They have tried to fit the concept of investing in individuals within the framework of traditional analysis. Within this framework, education, food, and shelter (both in physical units and in quality measurement) are inputs, and lifetime earnings are the output. Viewed in this manner, the productive process "reproduces" and "accumulates" people in the same way it invests and maintains physical capital. Final consumption, then, is merely an input, health expenditures are for maintaining the human machine, food is fuel, and so on.

There are those who find such an approach distasteful. One may cite no less a moral authority than John Stuart Mill to the effect that "The human being himself I do not classify as wealth. He is the purpose for which wealth exists."[20] The proponents of the human-capital closed-system approach would deny any implication of treating man only as a means toward great production. They

[20] Cited by J. Bonner and D. S. Lees, "Consumption and Investment," *Journal of Political Economy*, February 1963, p. 67.

say, rather, that all inputs and outputs should be considered and that there is good reason to believe that improvements in the quality of human beings have been a very important source of economic growth.[21] The advance of knowledge promoted by our educational system has made a major contribution to our performance. Denison, for example, has suggested:

> From 1929 to 1957 the amount of education the average worker had received was increasing almost two percent a year, and this was raising the average quality of labor by 0.97 percent per year, and contributing 0.67 percentage points to the growth rate of real national income.[22]

Abramovitz, Becker, Schultz, Weisbrod, and other economists have found education and other forms of investment in human capital to have a sizable impact on economic growth. They argue that there are strong reasons to believe that returns on investment in people may, from the purely economic standpoint, have a high rate of return.[23] It would be possible to collect statistical data which would describe what happens to some group or groups over time. A given age, sex, and racial group could be shown to have a certain probability of being unemployed—some percentage more or less than the average person in the population; the group could be shown as having an earning potential of X dollars. The data problems involved in constructing such tables would be severe, but they would show the extent of return on "investment in people."

Tracing members of the selected groups over time would prove both difficult and expensive. At the same time, it is of the utmost importance to know as precisely as possible the potentiality of subgroups within the population, and to be able to attribute to

---

[21] *Ibid.*

[22] Edward F. Denison, "Education, Economic Growth, and Gaps in Information," *Journal of Political Economy*, October 1962, p. 127.

[23] See Moses Abramovitz, "Economic Growth in the United States," *Journal of Political Economy*, December 1962; Gary Becker, *Human Capital* (New York: Columbia University Press, 1964); T. W. Schultz, "Investing in Poor People: An Economist's View," *American Economic Review*, May 1965; B. A. Weisbrod, "Investing in People," *Journal of Human Resources*, Summer 1966; and B. A. Weisbrod, "The Valuation of Human Capital," *Journal of Human Resources*, October 1961.

social or institutional forces the fact of poor performance in a competitive society. For if some are not given equal opportunity to compete effectively, then two things can be said to take place: (1) resources are not allocated as efficiently as they could be in the absence of the constraint on competition; and (2) individuals who are not provided with the same opportunity for "self-actualization"[24] (or the realization of their potential as creative human beings) are harmed systematically by societal discrimination. Indeed, both of these situations take place.

In 1962 the President's Council of Economic Advisers estimated that "if nonwhites had the same educational levels as whites and if the economy fully utilized their education, GNP today might be perhaps 3.2 percent higher."[25] In 1968 Barbara R. Bergmann reported that "the value of the stock of human capital embodied in the average male adult Negro is on the order of $10,000 smaller than the human capital the average white male has possession of. For the Nation as a whole, this adds up to a deficiency of around $50 million of investment in the human capital of adult male Negro Americans, which would have been made had they been whites."[26] Bergmann believes her measure to be "a rough and partial measure of what Negroes are 'owed' by American society."[27]

Knowing that blacks are systematically discriminated against is nothing new. The reality of being black has been chronicled in novels, plays, poetry, and scholarly tracts. The human-capital approach offers only one advantage. While others point to the existence and immorality of discriminatory practices, human-capital theorists stress their costs in dollars lost to the economy.

[24] See Gordon W. Allport, *Becoming: Basic Considerations for a Psychology of Personality* (New Haven: Yale University Press, 1955); and Abraham H. Maslow, *Motivation and Personality* (New York: Harper & Row, 1954).
[25] Council of Economic Advisers, "Economic Costs of Racial Discrimination in Employment," in *Economic Report of the President* (Washington, D.C.: Government Printing Office, September 1962).
[26] Barbara R. Bergmann, "Investment in the Human Resources of Negroes," in *Federal Programs for the Development of Human Resources, A Compendium of Papers Submitted to the Subcommittee on Economic Progress of the Joint Economic Committee, Congress of the United States* (Washington, D.C.: Government Printing Office, January 1968), p. 263.
[27] *Ibid.*, p. 266.

Understanding the Labor Market

It is impossible to comprehend the appeal George Wallace had in the 1968 presidential campaign without seeing that blacks represent a tremendous threat to many whites. White workers feel that their jobs are endangered by the blacks' demands for equality. They also see that programs to train blacks are being paid for by part of their rising taxes. The white working class fears a double loss; first, in competition for jobs, and second, in higher taxes to support government redistribution programs. Even if the new jobs are net increases, additional union members mean less overtime and fewer places that can go to the sons and nephews of white workers. These fears are not irrational but are founded on a rudimentary, yet accurate, understanding of the labor market.

The queuing theory of labor-market behavior suggests that employers attempt to hire the best qualified workers for a job by choosing those with the most experience, best training, and so on. Prospective employees are ranked. If there are twelve openings, the top dozen candidates are hired. Those at the end of the line will not get hired until the better candidates have jobs. This theory explains why blacks get hired more easily during periods of full employment; since all others are working, employers are forced to hire from the end of the queue. Using the 1954–1966 relationships, Lester Thurow has estimated that an increase of one percent in adult white male employment from 1968 levels would lead to an increase in adult nonwhite employment of 3.3 percent.[28] This would occur because less skilled and less experienced blacks are hired in tight labor markets, and employers who have discriminated on the basis of color find that in a near full-employment situation they pay too high a cost for this practice. Such a line of reasoning has led some economists to stress the importance of tight labor markets and of education.[29] With tight labor markets, white workers have less objection to the employment of blacks, even

[28] Lester Thurow, "Employment Gains and the Determinants of the Occupational Distribution of Negroes," in *Proceedings of a Conference on the Education and Training of Racial Minorities* (Madison, Wis.: University of Wisconsin Press, 1969).
[29] See Marshall, *The Negro Worker*, p. 158.

though education and work experience raise the capacity of blacks to compete for the existing jobs.

Matthew Edel has suggested the possibility that education changes the queuing order rather than merely raising productivity. In this case programs to educate the poor do not solve the employment-inflation dilemma. They leave instead the current underclass (largely nonwhite) facing the current employed (mostly white) in a zero-sum game. The white worker will be rationally (and perhaps also emotionally) racist if he opposes such programs.[30]

If blacks are enabled to compete on a stronger basis with whites for a fixed number of real jobs also desired by whites, programs will be resisted by white workers and their unions. In fact, education probably both upgrades black workers, enabling them to fill skilled job positions, and also gives those trained greater ability to compete against whites. If training is accompanied by a genuine commitment to full employment policies, through the federal government creating jobs, if necessary, there would be little, objectively, for whites to fear. Unfortunately, this country has been committed to full employment policies only in time of war.

While the queuing theory helps explain black underemployment and unemployment, it may be somewhat misleading. The queuing analysis suggests that those at the end of the hiring line are employed only in periods of full employment. This is not true. One study examining the labor force experience of those seeking help at a Boston employment center found:

> It appears that most ghetto workers are not perpetually out of work and unemployable. Although 85 percent of those entering ABCD's employment centers are unemployed when they apply, almost all have had quite recent work experience. Youths in the process of moving from school to work are virtually the only ones without a record of past employment.[31]

[30] Matthew Edel, "Economics for Social Change," Discussion Paper No. 2 (Ann Arbor, Mich.: The Union for Radical Political Economics, October 1968), p. 8.

[31] Penny H. Feldman, David M. Gordon, and Michael Reich, "Low-Income Labor Markets and Urban Manpower Programs: A Critical Assessment," Harvard Institute of Economic Research Discussion Paper No. 66, ed. Peter B. Doeringer (Cambridge, Mass.: Harvard University Press, February 1969), pp. 11–12.

Interviews with these unemployed indicated that most turnover was voluntary and caused by "low wages, the poor working conditions, and lack of advancement opportunities. These workers knew that such menial jobs are always available and that the accumulation of an erratic work history would not be a barrier to obtaining menial jobs in the future."[32] Findings of this nature have led some economists to suggest that the manpower problems of the ghetto are best seen in terms of *a dual labor market*.[33] The ghetto worker is confined to the secondary market where pay is low, work unpleasant and dull, promotion opportunities absent, and so on. The ghetto worker naturally has little commitment to such a job. In this he "puts no lower value on the job than does the larger society around him."[34]

The colonial analogy again is useful. There are in the colony jobs for natives and jobs for whites. "Nigger work" in the South gives way to exclusionary job classifications in the North. The principle at work is the same. Only in time of crisis, of labor shortage, are blacks in any number allowed to move into white jobs. The missionary promising the native salvation in the hereafter is replaced by the socializing arms of white society in the ghetto—the teachers and welfare workers. Aspirations of ghetto children are destroyed.[35] A few "show" blacks make it; most cannot.

The normal workings of the labor market discriminate against nonwhites in a number of ways. First, friends and relatives are the most common source of information about potential jobs, especially low-skilled requirement jobs. This places the black ghetto dweller at a disadvantage. More of the people he knows will be unemployed, or employed in unstable, low-paying jobs. There is less information to share, and what exists is for inferior jobs. Second, the very isolation of the ghetto makes job search more costly in terms of time and money than it might be for whites.

---

[32] *Ibid.*, p. 14.
[33] Michael J. Piore, "Public and Private Responsibility in On-the-Job Training of Disadvantaged Workers," pp. 2–3. Also see Feldman *et. al.*, "Low-Income Labor Markets," p. 50.
[34] Elliot Liebow, *Tally's Corner* (Boston: Little, Brown, 1967), p. 57.
[35] See Herbert Kohl, *36 Children* (New York: New American Library, 1967); and Robert Coles, *Children of Crisis: A Study in Courage and Fear* (Boston: Little, Brown, 1967).

Third, the job seeker's education and labor-force experience do not qualify him for a very wide range of jobs. Fourth, because the jobs he can get are low-paying and dull, he is likely not to hold a job for as long as he might if it were intrinsically more interesting or paid better. Finally, there is overt and covert discrimination by employers and unions.

Job Location Trends

From 1960 to 1966 white central-city population for the nation as a whole declined by 1.3 million.[36] At the same time there has been a concentration of new employment on the periphery of the cities. New construction of factories, commercial buildings, and a relatively large part of public buildings, as shown in the data on the value of building permits issued, is in suburban or periphery areas as opposed to central-city locations.[37] The growth of suburban rather than central-city employment has been commented upon by many social scientists, as has the high cost of transportation from central-city residence to suburban jobs. "There is substantial evidence that central city residents using public transport spend more money and time to reach suburban jobs than those commuting to the city."[38] The costs of travel must be measured in time and money. Low-wage jobs may act to discourage prospective workers from commuting very far. Some of the new suburban jobs are "subprofessional," "paratechnical"[39]—careers which seem especially suitable for the poor but are too far away from black residential areas. Even jobs traditionally held by blacks are moving to the suburbs, thus reducing opportunities for black workers.

There are black suburbanites, to be sure, but they are numerically a very small percentage of the black population. Also, as the suburban housing stock in some areas begins to show signs

[36] Cited in *Report of The National Advisory Committee on Civil Disorders* (New York: Bantam, 1968), p. 243.
[37] Dorothy K. Newman, "The Decentralization Jobs," *Monthly Labor Review*, May 1967, p. 7.
[38] *Ibid.*, p. 10.
[39] A. Pearl and F. Reisman, *New Careers for the Poor* (New York: The Free Press, 1969).

of age, a tendency has been noted, which should become increasingly evident over time, for whites to abandon certain older suburbs and for blacks to move in. This shift, of course, is usually accompanied by a general deterioration of public facilities and perhaps the subsequent creation of a suburban ghetto.

The extent to which housing segregation influences employment patterns has been tested by John Kain. Using as his variables the employment figures for nonwhites in each of a large number of workplaces in the metropolitan area, their distance from the nearest residence area with more than two percent nonwhite residents, and the distance from the workplace to the nearest point in the major ghetto, he ran multiple regressions for Detroit and Chicago.[40] Distance, as Kain suggests, is not as good an indicator of transportation costs as we might like, "because of the indirectness or complete absence of public transit services from ghetto residential areas to outlying or suburban workplaces."[41] Still, Kain's regressions suggest that "housing market segregation does strongly affect the location of Negro employment."[42]

The types of employment patterns Kain finds reinforce the effects of discriminatory housing practices. Not only are blacks underrepresented in employment as distance from the ghetto increases, but also, "Nonwhites are most overrepresented in those ghetto industries having the greatest amount of customer contact—retailing; finance, insurance and real estate; business services; and public administration. They are least overrepresented in those ghetto industries having the least customer contact—durable and nondurable manufacturing, wholesaling, and transportation. The converse seems to hold for Negro employment in all white areas."[43]

The data Kain presents for Chicago indicate that manufacturing jobs stayed relatively constant in number between 1950 and 1960 but were located, on the average, farther from the ghetto. The net result of residential patterns, migration rates, and net employment shifts by job type seems to be that "housing market segregation

[40] John F. Kain, "Housing Segregation, Negro Employment, and Metropolitan Decentralization," *Quarterly Journal of Economics*, May 1968, p. 180.
[41] *Ibid.*, pp. 180–81.
[42] *Ibid.*, p. 183.
[43] *Ibid.*, p. 187.

may reduce the level of Negro employment and, thereby, contribute to the high unemployment rates of metropolitan Negroes."[44]

Joseph Mooney has presented figures which show the percentage of jobs (in twenty-five of the largest metropolitan areas in the country) located in the central city to have fallen from 67.8 percent in 1948 to 59.2 percent in 1963. Those employment sectors which are growing (selected services, finance, insurance, and real estate) largely hire women. This situation partly reflects the desire of employers to seek women employees who can do the same work as men but who will work for less. One of the striking areas of retrogression over these same years is the status of the black family. The number of families headed by females continues to rise. The job situation in the central city *for males* does not show much promise.[45]

Residential segregation contributes not only to ghetto unemployment and the breakup of black families, but also to the "crises" in urban transportation and finance, and the creation of the "white garrison suburbs." It is interesting to note in this regard that the subsidies going to commuter railroads like the Long Island and the Skokie line help high-income commuters. The executives who ride these subsidized lines are rarely subject to the cattle-train conditions of the inner-city rush-hour mass transit. Even the new systems such as the San Francisco Bay Area Rapid Transit commuter line will be of little assistance to city residents. Systems being planned for Los Angeles and Atlanta will follow a similar pattern of helping the suburbanites and giving only marginal assistance to the urban poor.

Policy Proposals for Job-Creation and Manpower Training for Ghetto Workers

How can the black employment situation be improved? Three approaches are currently being attempted: increasing the effective-

---

[44] *Ibid.*
[45] Joseph D. Mooney, "Housing Segregation, Negro Employment, and Metropolitan Decentralization: An Alternative Prospect," *Quarterly Journal of Economics*, May 1969, p. 311.

ness of market forces, subsidizing preferred patterns at the margin, and upgrading the urban subemployed labor force. After presenting each we shall discuss why they have been of such limited success.

Increasing the effectiveness of labor markets has many dimensions. Traditionally, attention has focused on making information concerning job openings available to ghetto residents. Much more important are efforts to allow blacks access to available jobs. An enforcement of existing open occupancy laws, combined with subsidized home-ownership loans, would enable blacks to move out to the suburbs where jobs are opening up in great numbers. To do this will take federal, state, or regional authority willing and able to override local restrictive practices. Here, as in so many other areas, one must first have major changes in power relations before meaningful social policy programs can be effectively implemented. One tactical expedient worth trying is the time-honored American practice of bribery—or as the economist would say, "subsidizing preferred patterns at the margin."

If the objective is to integrate housing, a subsidy can be paid to blacks who move into predominantly white neighbohoods, and whites who move into black neighborhoods. Subsidies could be paid of ten or fifteen percent of the cost of housing (purchase price, or rental for some specified period). The amount of subsidy could be increased if it were not enough to induce movement. The subsidy could be withdrawn once racial mix came within a fixed range of the area-wide racial composition. Additional subsidies could be paid to suburban areas receiving poorer immigrants (for example, payment of the full cost of educating the children of the new family).[46]

In the same fashion, in the inner city, hard-core unemployed could be certified and employers hiring them be given wage subsidies based on a scale which increases with the duration of previous unemployment and decreases with the length of time on the new job. The first is a proxy for the worker's lack of marketable skills; the second for increases in his productivity which come from con-

---

[46] See Ira S. Lowry, "Housing," in *Cities in Trouble: An Agenda for Urban Research*, ed. Anthony H. Pascal (Santa Monica, Calif.: The Rand Corporation, 1968), pp. 24–25.

tinued employment. Subsidy schedules could be raised or lowered to correspond to area-wide changes in unemployment rates.[47]

Given the current climate of opinion, there would be great opposition from taxpayers to helping one group which had not "earned" jobs (or good housing). "We worked for it, let them." This attitude is pervasive among whites.

The justification for such subsidies comes from the existence of the matrix of problems faced by blacks, the systematic discrimination of the labor market being just one manifestation of the society's racism. A white man is judged as a man, on his individual merits; a black is stereotyped as a black and judged undesirable. This reality is denied by the very workers whose unions exclude blacks from membership.[48] The complaint that taxes out of the general revenue are being spent to help one specially privileged group can, of course, just as easily be raised against oil depletion allowances, subsidies to United States shipbuilders, and tariffs to protect domestic products. Such groups can, fortunately for them, afford lobbyists in Washington, high-priced lawyers, and public-relations firms to help secure special treatment.

The federal government's Manpower Development and Training Program has received popular approval,[49] in part because education and training seem to be ways to "help the poor help them-

---

[47] A program of this kind has been suggested by John F. Kain. See his "Coping with Ghetto Unemployment," *Program on Regional and Urban Economics*, Harvard University Discussion Paper No. 40 (Cambridge, Mass.: Harvard University Press, November 1968); and the same author's, "Coping with Ghetto Unemployment," *Journal of the American Institute of Planners*, March 1969.

[48] The following sentences appeared in a newspaper article on the day this chapter was written: "BOSTON. One day last month, the United Community Construction Workers, an organization of about 350 Negroes, sent a 'black tester' to five Federally funded construction jobs that were reported to be experiencing a labor shortage. The tester, a carpenter with five years' experience, was turned down at all five sites, according to a spokesman for the Urban League, because employment was controlled, with the consent of the contractors, by a predominantly white building trades union." *The New York Times*, April 3, 1969, p. 1.

[49] These programs are reviewed in U.S. Department of Labor, *A Report on Manpower Requirements, Resources, Utilization, and Training*; and in Garth L. Mangum, *Contributions and Costs of Manpower Development and Training* (Ann Arbor, Mich.: Institute of Labor and Industrial Relations, 1967).

selves," and partly because training in this program has rarely been tied to job openings where blacks can compete with whites, after they are trained, for desirable positions. The program does not interfere with vested interests. Workers are trained only for jobs where there are labor shortages. Hence, employers are happy, since their labor needs are better met at no cost to the firms involved. Unions accept the program, for the jobs held by their members are not endangered. Of course, the vacant jobs are generally unfilled because they are unattractive. In other cases jobs are unfilled because of labor union or employment policy, and it is unlikely that the newly trained will find jobs upon completion of their program. It is still useful to discuss ways in which the program can be improved, even though, for reasons we shall discuss later on, the framework of such programs is inadequate.

Manpower programs have four constituent parts: recruiting, training, placing, and counseling. Each of these requires hard policy choices in how best to serve the ghetto unemployed.

First, recruiting involves reaching out to those who have become cynical about the white society's desire to really give them a chance. Advertisements in the "white" press and on "white" radio stations, for example, will not be as successful in reaching people as the same advertisements in media which serve the black community (or the Mexican-American, Indian, or Puerto Rican communities, to which this discussion applies as well). Another type of decision concerns itself with those the program should seek to reach. Is the attempt being made to reach those who are most in need of help? If so, program failure rates will be higher than if the more trainable are accepted. If trying to run up a good score is the aim, in order to gain public and congressional acceptance for the program, then the risk is run of serving those who would have found jobs even without the program.

Second, training is probably also best achieved if the teacher is most sympathetic to the trainees. Where training is done on the job, a buddy system has proved successful when the older, more experienced worker is given a strong incentive to help the new worker learn the ropes. A bonus of, say, $1,000 to the worker of immigrant stock if the young black he is coaching stays on the job successfully for a year is a use of the profit motive that would seem well worth trying. A more successful adjustment to the work routine might also be possible if new workers with poor or nonexistent labor force experience were first trained in special plants—feeder factories—where work habits and skills could be learned in more controlled conditions. Once strong work attitudes and skills were developed, the worker could be placed elsewhere. There is also the question of what the stress in training should be. When the training is too specialized, say bricklaying or welding, then if these specialized jobs are not available or if workers are laid off, investment has been made in a skill which is not easily transferable. In addition, many applicants for job training are so far behind in reading ability or elementary mathematics that they cannot read training manuals and follow instruction booklets. A more general remedial training may be very necessary for some workers.

Placement is a problem in that the worker, even after training, is competing against job applicants who are better trained and more highly qualified. This will be especially true of higher-paying jobs. In such cases, perhaps wage supplements should be considered for some transitional period to compensate employers for the lower productivity of the new workers. The government could go further and stipulate that when a firm receives a government contract, it must fill X percent of its new job openings from the pool of recently trained ghetto residents. In federal and local government jobs, ghetto residents could be given some advantage in bonus points, as are given to veterans. The rationale for the special treatment of veterans is that the men served their country. Ghetto residents could be given points because the society has handicapped them by allowing them only an inferior education and because of the overt personal, as well as institutional, racism to which they are subjected. Certainly there can be no equality of opportunity until all citizens are given the same preparation for the job market.

Finally, counseling can be very important for the ghetto resident who breaks the barrier and finds employment alongside white workers. Every black is not a Jackie Robinson, able to suffer abuse and stick it out through sheer guts and skill. The average and less-than-average in ability must be helped to get and hold the jobs that whites of average and below-average ability hold. Counseling will help people hold jobs, but as Doeringer has commented, "The problem of excessive turnover has generally evaded solution, except as a by-product of placement on higher wage, or otherwise more desirable jobs."[50]

It may also be necessary to change the ghetto dweller's attitude toward work. However, a change in attitude is possible only if there is simultaneously a change in the worker's reality as he sees it—that is, if a job ladder is available to the worker and he sees real chance for self-improvement. Marc Fried has put the matter in terms of a hierarchy of work orientation where one first must learn to conform to the requirements and discipline of the workplace, then learn to view work with the pride of mastery of skills. At a higher level still, work becomes pleasurable in that the worker develops responsibility for an entire work objective; he has an "occupation" as opposed to a "job." Finally, at the highest level, work becomes a career, wherein personal achievement is identified with occupational role, and advancement brings an increased sense of personal development.[51]

Certainly, it is at this stage utopian to expect all men to view work as a career. This is not possible for the majority of jobs as they are currently structured. And yet it is just this restructuring which is really what black youths are demanding. Dan Aldridge's view is that

> The revolt of these young people against this racist-capitalist system is not about to cease, not because these brothers are incapable of doing many of the jobs that people have for them, but because they are already so politically conscious and their understanding so deep that they are not challenged by these jobs. The work involved is not meaningful enough to these brothers to justify their spending eight hours a day in the sweatshops, regardless of the wages they receive.[52]

[50] Peter B. Doeringer, "Ghetto Labor Markets—Problems and Programs," *Program on Regional and Urban Economics*, No. 35 (Cambridge, Mass.: Harvard University Press, May 1968), p. 17.
[51] Marc A. Fried, "The Role of Work in a Mobile Society," in Sam Bass Warner, ed., *Planning for a Nation of Cities* (Cambridge, Mass.: The M.I.T. Press, 1966), especially pp. 85–87.
[52] Dan Aldridge, "Politics in Command of Economics: Black Economic Development," a speech given at the National Black Economic Development Conference in April 1969. Published in a revised version, *Monthly Review*, November 1969, p. 22.

He defines challenging and meaningful work as jobs that will "increase our political consciousness and our sense of social, responsibility and make our relationship to our own people a closer one and make us more aware of what we can do to further our liberation—if we can't have such jobs, then we don't want to work."[53] Blacks in increasing numbers are realizing that what they are being offered is a restricted place at the bottom of the job ladder. A *job* is offered—not an occupation and not a career. To offer a career is to begin with the man and discover how he might best contribute to the society.

Education, training, and work attitudes are relative matters. For this reason, truly universal education of a high quality would upset long-sustained social relations. The nature of American development has created an underclass in this country which has been kept ignorant to serve in the least desirable labor force roles. A different pattern of growth could remake our society. Full employment without inflation could go far to do away with the underclass. Keyserling has noted, "During World War II, we reduced unemployment to less than one million. Now we have full-time unemployment of more than four million. It would be dangerous nonsense to think that the number of shiftless or otherwise unfit people has multiplied four times in the intervening years."[54] A real war on poverty could create the same conditions. An increase in the number of jobs available, through fulfilling the demand for goods and services in the public sector, would create employment opportunities for ghetto workers. Especially if white workers were convinced that the commitment to full employment and social reconstruction were permanent, they would be willing to let blacks into unions. Such a program need not make the government the "employer of last resort," hiring all those who need jobs; rather the aim would be to "make the public jobs an integral part of the labor market, available to any workers who prefer them, forcing employers to outbid the government for their labor, and recognizing and accepting the inflationary impact that would follow. The effects would be similar to, and probably of a magnitude no

[53] *Ibid.*
[54] Leon H. Keyserling, *Progress or Poverty* (Washington, D.C.: Conference on Economic Progress, 1964), p. 14.

greater than, those experienced each time the statutory minimum wage is raised."[55]

The trouble with the war on poverty, besides its token appropriations and lack of serious government commitment, was that while the objectives were radical, the means were essentially conservative. There was no effort made to achieve the elimination of poverty through the direct creation of useful work.[56] Moreover, when all is said and done about the workings of the labor market and the welfare system, the question becomes not "what can be done?" but rather "how do we do what we know must be done?" There is no end of useful suggestions. Economists are creative enough to design subsidy schemes which are technically sound, and plans capable of bringing minority groups into roles as participants in meaningful ways in the economy. Resistance to such changes, however, prevents implementing progressive programs on a scale necessary to alter significantly the present reality. The pressing concern of social scientists therefore becomes power relations and how these can be changed. The economist has another, and equally important, question to explore. To what extent does the American economy, and capitalist economies in general, need the functional equivalent of black people? It may well be that a meaningful war on poverty is held up not merely by prior commitments, military and other, or by the resistance of voters, but more fundamentally because the economy needs "niggers."

Having described the place the black ghetto occupies in the American economy and the mechanisms through which this status is maintained, we must examine alternative strategies for change. This task is discharged in the next and last chapter.

[55] James L. Sundquist, "Jobs, Training, and Welfare for the Underclass," in *Agenda for the Nation*, ed. Kermit Gordon (Washington, D.C.: The Brookings Institution, 1968), p. 61.
[56] *Ibid.*

CHAPTER 7

Alternative Goals and Strategies of Social Change

The converging crises of race relations and the city have been the subject of countless Sunday supplements and television specials. The concentration of the poor in the central city and the wealthy in the suburbs creates housing and employment problems. The schools, hospitals, and courts cannot cope with the demands put upon them. Congestion, pollution, and crime are major social problems. "Such issues affect all Americans regardless of race or income. Something must be done."

The view from the ghetto is, as we have seen, somewhat different. The exploitation of blacks is nothing new. Housing has always been inferior, wages below whites', discrimination of "crisis" proportions. There is nothing unique in the present situation. What is new is that it is becoming increasingly clear that always putting private profit ahead of social need hurts whites as well as blacks. So attempts are being made to patch things up.

What is also new is that blacks, increasingly concentrated in central cities, see that change is possible if they fight for it, and that appeals for justice are not nearly so effective as black-

129

organized and black-led struggles to force concessions. Blacks see that they must organize and struggle not as individuals but as a group, because that is the way white society sees them.

Forced segregation is an *increasing* reality. As Anthony Downs has written, "All evidence points to the conclusion that future non-white population growth will continue to be concentrated in central cities unless major changes in public policies are made. Not one single significant program of any federal, state, or local government is aimed at altering this tendency or is likely to have the unintended effect of doing so."[1] Given such trends, the cities cannot be made better for whites unless they are made better for blacks. Isolation is possible when the ghetto is small and can be ignored. As the ghetto grows to surround the downtown business districts and the upper-income neighborhoods and reaches the very borders of white suburbia, whites will find it increasingly difficult to enjoy their preferential position unless policies for urban improvement include proposals to help the ghetto.

The Timing and the Direction of Social Change

The pressure of black militancy has led to discussion of how best to prevent violence. This is not the same as asking how to end the status of second-class citizenship "enjoyed" by blacks. The best way to end ghetto insurrection would be to stop the colonial exploitation of black workers and to use the resources of society to develop human potential. This approach is rarely considered, except rhetorically, because to implement it would take fundamental changes in basic institutions and attitudes. It would hit the purse of the wealthy. This is obvious and yet important to reiterate because the narrow framework of most programs of reform makes them palliatives to calm, not programs for change.

There is a consensus in the liberal sections of the corporate community that something must be done about the urban crisis. This new involvement does not reflect a changed ideology. Corporate leaders are still committed to low taxes and minimal government intervention in general, but strong self-interest in preserving

[1] Anthony Downs, "Alternative Futures for the American Ghetto," *Daedalus*, Fall 1968, p. 1333.

assets of city-based operations leads them to want more effective government planning and greater financial investment in urban facilities. It is perfectly reasonable, then, that in the crusade to alleviate urban problems "the strongest support came from a part of the community which the casual observer might have considered the least ready for it—the merchants, the financiers, and the daily press, whose ideology seemed almost unqualifiedly committed to the proposition that the interference of government in the economic affairs of men was unwise and unproductive."[2] The metropolitan-based corporations are seeking more federal expenditures in urban areas, channeled through the private sector, in order to protect their own investments—a sort of private-interest socialism. While such programs may be in the short-run interests of the private sector, they are not desirable, as we have suggested earlier, from the point of view of the ghetto. As social scientists have long pointed out, real change will come with programs which recognize the interrelatedness of problems and formulate a multi-dimensional approach to their solution.

The cost of such comprehensive programs is great indeed when considered against what we are currently spending. They call for a reorientation of priorities and, as a working principle of societal organization, placement of social need ahead of private profit. This has not always been so. In earlier years smaller concessions would have been acceptable, but, because white society has refused to grant very much, blacks have grown cynical of white motives and upped the ante on what they are asking. The early civil rights movement wanted equal opportunity for personal advancement; today blacks understand that the way this society "gives them a chance" ensures a high individual failure rate.

Martin Duberman has reminded us that the view of the militants has changed since the early sixties. "The only kind of progressive coalition which can exist in this country, they [the militants] say, is the mild, liberal variety which produced the civil rights legislation of recent years. And that kind of legislation has proven itself grossly inadequate. Its chief result has been to lull white liberals

[2] Raymond Vernon, "The Myth and Reality of Our Urban Problems," in *City and Suburb: The Economics of Metropolitan Growth*, ed. Benjamin Chinitz (Englewood Cliffs, N.J.: Prentice-Hall, 1964), p. 98.

into believing that the major battles have been won, whereas in fact there has been almost no change, or change for the worse, in the daily lives of most blacks. . . . The legislation produced by the liberal coalition of the early sixties has turned out to be little more than federally approved tokenism, a continuation of paper promises and ancient inequities."[3] Radicalism comes from failure of reform and awareness that meaningful change of basically evil institutions is not possible.

SNCC, after all, did not start with a philosophy of black power. It began as an interracial movement, with a religious orientation "committed to the 'American Dream.' "[4] When the most elementary rights were denied, SNCC grew more hostile to white society and came to the view that blacks must organize alone, that white liberals were not really committed but would always settle for token gains. The civil rights legislation which many Americans have taken pride in passing in the 1960s was in reality much more conservative than that passed more than a hundred years ago. The Civil Rights Act of 1866, still on the books, declares, "All citizens of the United States shall have the same right, in every state and territory, as is enjoyed by white citizens thereof, to inherit, purchase, lease, sell, hold, and convey real and personal property.[5] For a hundred years, what has been lacking is enough commitment to "law and order" to enforce such legislation. Who is to say that the militants have been wrong in their judgment of white willingness to end racism? Countless cases can be cited of federal court orders being ignored, of agency heads being let go for too actively pursuing integrationist goals. For instance, *The Wall Street Journal* of July 22, 1969, reported "GO SLOW" signs flashing at the Federal Equal Employment Opportunity Commission after its head was fired at the insistence of the late Senator Everett Dirksen and other conservatives who claimed EEOC "harassment" of corporations. The new commission head "decides against holding further public hearings to question employers about their hiring practices; he favors 'private conferences.' " Newspaper accounts periodically speak of pressures on other federal agencies which are overzealous

[3] Martin Duberman, "Black Power in America," *Partisan Review*, Winter 1968, p. 38.
[4] *Ibid.*, p. 41.
[5] See Clair Wilcox, *Toward Social Policy* (Homewood, Ill.: Richard D. Irwin, 1969), Chapter 12, especially p. 203.

in enforcing the law of the land. It is no wonder that blacks lose patience. Part of the real function of positive-sounding statements from government officials is to attempt merely to take the pressure off. One thing militants fear more than repression is co-optation. From this cynical viewpoint, liberalism appears an enemy of meaningful social change. Consider the following four terms: demonstration project, tokenism, paternalism, and study commission.

A Short Dictionary of Liberalism

A demonstration program, in the words of some anonymous Washington cynic, is "a way of looking like you are doing something while doing nothing." Demonstration programs logically flow from the need for research to be done so that large sums of money will not be committed in wasteful ways. Some demonstrations do work: feed school children nourishing meals, and they do become healthier and perform better in school; teach ghetto youths the skills through on-the-job training programs, and they do become able to hold jobs; and so on. However, when demonstrations succeed they are hardly ever expanded on a wide basis with adequate funding. What results, instead, is the establishment of a token program. Tokenism is a step down from a demonstration project. Annual funding provides just enough to keep a staff of bureaucrats paid with not much left over for programs. The few government programs which do receive generous funding serve, as was suggested earlier, the not-so-poor. When funds go to help the poor, government programs are traditionally paternalistic, meaning simply that they breed and reinforce dependency. The group that has been longest under the care of the United States government is the American Indian. After pacification, his land was taken and he was segregated on reservations and cared for by the Bureau of Indian Affairs. Having been looked after the longest, the Indian is the worst off of any group. "He suffers most from malnutrition and disease; his death rate is 70 percent above that of the general population; his life-span is only 42 years. He has the poorest housing: nine tenths of it is below the minimum standards of safety, health, and decency. He is the least educated: his literacy rate is only 50 percent. He has the least secure employment: his unemployment rate is seven times the national average. He is in the deepest poverty: his average family income in 1962 was $1,500, only half of the figure then taken as the poverty line."[6] If this is the way white society compensates a people whom it has systematically robbed and murdered, why should blacks expect more generosity? The ghetto takes on more and more of the trappings of an urban reservation.

The final term to be considered is the study commission. Most famous of these is, of course, the Kerner Commission, which found America to be racist. The Kerner Commission described deprivation and black resentment of white oppression as the long-run causes of rebellion, and the behavior of the white armies of occupation—the police, who often trigger the final incident before the outbreak of violence—as the short-run cause. Commission findings are never anything new. As Kenneth Clark said before the Kerner Commission, "I read that report . . . of the 1919 riot in Chicago, and it is as if I were reading the report of the investigating committee on the Harlem riot of 1935, the report of the investigating committee on the Harlem riot of 1943, the report of the McCone Commission on the Watts riot. I must again in candor say to you members of this Commission—it is a kind of Alice in Wonderland with the same moving picture re-shown over and over again, the same analysis, the same recommendations, and the same inaction."[7]

The purpose of the study commission is the same as the function of a demonstration project—to quiet opposition and public concern by promising research which will lead to change. After the research is done, enough time has passed so that the pressure is off. This is not to say that commissions do not come up with useful reports. They may. When they do, however, there is no guarantee that their recommendations will be heeded. The constructive proposals of the Kerner Commission have been ignored by the president who appointed it and by his successor.

[6] *Ibid.*, p. 52.
[7] The National Advisory Commission on Civil Disorders, *Report of The National Advisory Commission on Civil Disorders* (New York: Bantam, 1968), p. 29.

Goals of Social Policy

There seem to be three versions of the future possible for the ghetto. First, present policies can be continued. We implicitly make this choice if we do not change the current direction of social policy. It leads to race warfare and urban *apartheid*. In the famous words of the Kerner Commission: "Our nation is moving toward two societies, one black, one white—separate and unequal."[8] Second, the ghetto can be rehabilitated, strengthened, enriched. Third, the ghetto can be opened and the society be made one rather than two nations. The third is the policy traditionally advocated. It entails ending segregated living arrangements and job discrimination, and investing adequately in health, education, and job training. Such a strategy would not mean an end to black communities but rather freedom of choice for black residents as to where they wish to live. Such a policy, while accepted by more Americans today than in the past, is not being carried out with anything like "all deliberate speed." As we have suggested, the reverse may be true in large metropolitan areas.

An integrationist strategy would help the ghetto by taking some of the pressure off overcrowded schools, and would lead to less demand for ghetto housing, and so to lower rents, or at least to rents more in line with those paid for similar accommodations elsewhere. Recent trends toward increasing segregation can be reversed only through radically different programs and rigorous application of old ones. Open housing laws, even if scrupulously enforced, would be merely a start. Economists have suggested ownership supplements, low-cost loans, and rent subsidies to assist low-income people in obtaining suburban housing. Further incentives should be given to the suburbs to encourage them to accept ghetto dwellers. Anthony Downs suggests school-support bonus payments linked to the education of children moving out from ghettos, and other devices which essentially attach a subsidy to a person. Then, when the person moves, he and the community into which he goes get credit for that subsidy. This creates incen-

[8] *Ibid.*, p. 1.

tives both for him to move and for the community to accept him gladly.[9]

Enrichment of the ghetto has been criticized from two vantage points; while getting rid of rats, building better housing, and improving public services are all well and good, rehabilitation "has the disadvantage of embalming the ghetto and its status as an area of involuntary confinement. As long as confinement exists, oppression exists, however clean the streets and habitable the home."[10]

Kain and Persky argue that "as long as the ghetto exists, most of white America will write off the central city"—and this means the inevitable decline of the city. They write: " 'Gilding' programs must accept as given a continued growth of Negro ghettos, ghettos which are directly or indirectly responsible for the failure of urban renewal, the crisis in central city finance, urban transportation problems, Negro unemployment, and the inadequacy of metropolitan school systems. Ghetto gilding programs, apart from being objectionable on moral grounds, accept a very large cost in terms of economic inefficiency, while making the solution of many social problems inordinately difficult."[11]

The view that the ghettos have been held in colony-like subjugation by the white society has a counterpart in visualizing as neo-colonialism development of the ghetto by large outside corporations. Independence would require possession of real power— power commensurate with the numerical strength of the black people in this country. Economic development which resulted from local initiative, organization, and control could create true independence. Barry Bluestone writes, "While the creation of a black economy in the ghetto may not lead inexorably to a viable economic base—competitive with the staunchest of 'white' enterprise—the act of striving toward an inner city economy yields a powerful tool for organizing the black community into a coherent political force capable of extracting concessions on jobs, housing, income, and dignity from the government and from the corporate

[9] Downs, "Alternative Futures for the American Ghetto," p. 1351.
[10] Kenneth B. Clark, "The Negro and the Urban Crisis," in *Agenda for the Nation*, ed. Kermit Gordon (Washington, D.C.: The Brookings Institution, 1968), p. 129.
[11] John F. Kain and Joseph J. Persky, "Alternatives to the Gilded Ghetto," *The Public Interest*, Winter 1969, p. 86.

establishment."[12] Just as many new nations who were "given" independence have not shown as much development as those which became independent in long struggles involving great masses of people, so the ghetto that is given the "war on poverty" largess is not likely to develop as well as the ghetto which can organize its own black economic development strategy and see it through.

Ghetto development has been criticized by many because it is feared that such a policy would lead to separatism, and because it is an economically unsound approach. "In the short run, the argument for ghetto improvement would have us view the ghetto as something of a community unto itself, a community that could substantially benefit from economic development and especially heavy investments of physical capital," say Kain and Persky.[13] But this, they argue, is a misleading analysis. The central city is poor *because* it is inhabited so heavily by blacks, who are restricted to the central city not because of income but because of discrimination. For example, "45 percent of Detroit's poor white families live in the suburbs, but only 11 percent of its poor Negro families do."[14] But again, this merely underscores the lack of political power. It does not speak to the question of *how* white racism can be overcome. Separatism to the extent that it creates political strength is a means of achieving eventual integration.

Obstacles to Change

There are two difficulties in accomplishing meaningful social change. First, there is a false consciousness among both whites and blacks which does not allow them to think in terms of fundamental change. While granting the justness of the black freedom struggle, they urge slowness and moderation. Bayard Rustin has captured this sense of "intelligent moderation" which inhibits meaningful progress. He writes:

[12] Barry Bluestone, "Black Capitalism: The Path to Black Liberation?" *The Review of Radical Economics* (Ann Arbor, Mich.: The Union for Radical Political Economics, May 1969), p. 53.
[13] Kain and Persky, "Alternatives to the Gilded Ghetto," p. 75.
[14] *Ibid.*

"Thus, during the first New York school boycott, *The New York Times* editorialized that Negro demands, while abstractly just, would necessitate massive reforms, the funds for which could not realistically be anticipated; therefore the just demands were also foolish demands and would only antagonize white people. Moderates of this stripe are often correct in perceiving the difficulty or impossibility of racial progress in the context of present social and economic policies. But they accept the context as fixed. . . . They apparently see nothing strange in the fact that in the last twenty-five years we have spent nearly a trillion dollars fighting or preparing for wars, yet throw up our hands before the need for overhauling our schools, clearing the slums, and really abolishing poverty. My quarrel with these moderates is that they do not even envision radical change; their admonitions of moderation are, for all practical purposes, admonitions to the Negro to adjust to the status quo, and are therefore immoral."[15]

The constraints of self-imposed limits on acceptable forms and degrees of social change are not themselves a fixed and inexplicable datum. The defense and space programs are accepted by Americans because those who profit from them convince us we need them. This is not the place for an extended treatment of the relation between government and industry. But some brief comments should be made.

The Role of the Corporate Sector

The competitive system we live under does not allow for the expenditure of significant sums of money by corporations on socially useful but privately unprofitable purposes. "The low economic status of Negroes, it must be noted, could be radically changed in short order if the 2,000 or so men who control the major American corporations really desired such changes."[16] At one level this is true; the corporations these men run could hire

[15] Bayard Rustin, "From Protest to Politics: The Future of the Civil Rights Movement," in *Urban Planning and Social Policy*, ed. B. J. Frieden and Robert Morris (New York: Basic Books, 1968), pp. 339–40.
[16] Gabriel Kolko, *Wealth and Power in America* (New York: Praeger, 1962), p. 109.

and train blacks to hold meaningful jobs, they could build good integrated housing for their labor force, they could pump money into company-financed high-quality schools for the communities in which they have plants (or use corporate influence to see that the government does these things). Such behavior would be a departure from past corporation practices. Any generosity shown workers has been either to gain greater control over their loyalties, or as a result of worker pressure.

If any single corporation president were to wake up tomorrow committed to spending one half of the company's profits in the cause of the economic advancement of blacks, he would be voted out by his stockholders. If he owned the company himself he would find his competitive position quickly slipping. To expect privately owned corporations to commit sizable resources to ghetto development seems unrealistic. By 1970 the glamour of urban involvement had worn off. A survey, published in the *Harvard Business Review,* of the urban affairs programs of 247 large corporations showed that top management is dissatisfied with the results of these programs and is cutting back on funding.[17] These firms were motivated to become involved in urban activities for a number of reasons, the most important of which, according to this survey, was "appearance." For "four fifths of the companies strengthening corporate reputation and image is a key objective."[18] The factor rated second in importance was compliance with the law. This was stressed especially by firms doing business with the government. "One executive said flatly, 'Our policy against discrimination was adopted in response to the law—not conscience, civic spirit, or sentiment.' "[19] A third of the firms said their participation was taken as insurance against boycotts and violence. Only a small proportion of the respondents (one eighth) were "explicitly interested in opening up new markets by attracting minority group customers or in selling their services as trainers or consultants to government or other companies."[20]

In this group of large corporations as a whole, there was a feel-

---

[17] Jules Cohn, "Is Business Meeting the Challenge of Urban Affairs?" *Harvard Business Review*, March–April 1970.
[18] *Ibid.*, p. 70.
[19] *Ibid.*
[20] *Ibid.*

ing that in the wake of the 1967 riots they may have "acted too impulsively," getting as involved as they did. "After the relatively 'cool' summers of 1968 and 1969, public and government pressure on corporations to act to ameliorate the urban crisis had somewhat diminished."[21] Also, costs had been more than many corporate officials had anticipated. Summarizing his findings, the investigator reported: "They jumped on the urban affairs bandwagon two years ago but many of them got off. . . . They're facing the fact that this area is possibly not germane to them and they're going back to the position they've had all along—business is really business."[22] The lesson seems to be that these corporations were not really interested in peace and freedom, but rather in peace and quiet, and when the riots lessened in frequency and intensity they turned their attention to more important matters. As one executive put it: "We serve our social function by increasing earnings per share."[23] If the corporations are to be involved it will mean giving them much stronger financial incentives or bringing them under social control.

Corporate incentives are more costly than a direct program of government rebuilding of the cities, enforcement of anti-discrimination and equal opportunity legislation. But the government is no more willing to change priorities than is industry. Carol Brightman reminds us, "The decisions which ghettoized the black community were not made by black people, but by the national elites who have chosen to maximize technological development at the expense of social development. America's inner cities suffer less from neglect than from the nature of their integration into both the local and national political economies."[24]

The nature of the blacks' relation to white society, we have suggested, is essentially that of a colony controlled and manipulated by the dominant society. The plight of the ghetto is partly a question of priorities (private profit before social need) and in part a matter of direct self-interest (the gains to be made through the historic exploitation of unorganized black labor). The program of

[21] *Ibid.*, p. 69.
[22] Quoted in Leonard Sloane, "Businesses Cut Back Urban Funds," *The New York Times*, March 1, 1970, p. 57.
[23] Cohn, "Is Business Meeting the Challenge of Urban Affairs?" p. 70.
[24] Carol Brightman, "The Dynamics of American Racism," *Viet-Report*, Summer 1968, p. 6.

Black Power flows from this awareness. Earl Raab has suggested that this is "the staple of Black Anger: if the American society did it to us deliberately, and admits having done it to us, then reparations are due—and now, not opportunity but reparations. Such reparations don't call for some 'natural process' of advancement, but for a compensatory 'leap forward' of a kind which has never taken place in the American society."[25] We now turn to the nature of the compensation being asked for, and the equally important question of the extent to which these demands represent potential for revolutionary change in America.

Black Priorities

The outlines of the kinds of changes being demanded seem clear enough. First, there is the demand for black control over the black community—over its public institutions such as the schools, the police and fire departments, and over its economy, resulting in black-owned businesses and/or cooperative black ownership. Second, there is the demand for a program to be sponsored by the federal government and modeled on the WPA, to create jobs at decent wages for all who need them. Commenting on such a proposal, Huberman and Sweezy suggest that "projects should be designed to employ people as they are—skilled and unskilled, educated and uneducated, old and young, artists and ditchdiggers—and they should be aimed at meeting the real needs of the ghettos and slums. These include rehabilitation of existing housing, building of new housing, creation and staffing of day-care centers for children, cleaning up vacant land, making playgrounds and parks, and so on *ad infinitum*. Like the WPA during the 1930's, this program should be financed by the federal government, but administration should be radically decentralized."[26]

A third type of demand is embodied in the "Black Manifesto"

[25] Earl Raab, "A Renewed Perspective on Urban Problems," in *Contributions to the Analysis of Urban Problems*, ed. Anthony H. Pascal (Santa Monica, Calif.: The Rand Corporation, 1968), p. 7.
[26] Leo Huberman and Paul M. Sweezy, "Reform and Revolution," *Monthly Review*, June 1968, p. 8.

presented to the white churches of America in 1969 by a group of blacks headed by James Forman. The manifesto called for reparations of a half billion dollars as compensation for the "centuries we have been forced to live as colonized people inside the United States."[27] The reparations are to go toward building black ability to make further demands on the white society and to fund institutions which could in themselves improve the standard of living of black Americans. In the first category are demands for the establishment of a black-owned publishing and printing industry, audio-visual networks, research centers, a training center for community organization, a black university, a "national Black Labor Strike and Defense Fund," and special funds to organize welfare people. In the second classification are a southern land bank to found cooperatives, and the establishment of cooperative businesses in the United States and Africa. These demands are predicated on the recognition of white blame for black deprivation. They not only ask that blacks be given equal opportunity, but that they also be given the wherewithal to insure equality of achievement, the resources to provide not just low-paying work, but good, well-paying, creative work.

The economic philosophy embodied in such proposals has been enunciated by Robert L. Allen:

> If the community as a whole is to benefit, then *the community as a whole must be organized to manage collectively* its internal economy and its business relations with white America. Black business firms must be treated and operated as *social property*, belonging to the general black community, not as the private property of individual or limited groups of individuals. This necessitates the dismantling of capitalist property relations in the black community and their replacement with a planned communal economy.[28]

Demands such as these are resisted. Their acceptance would threaten the privileges enjoyed by white society at the expense of blacks.

[27] *The New York Review of Books*, July 10, 1969, p. 32.
[28] Robert L. Allen, *Black Awakening in Capitalist America: An Analytic History* (Garden City, N.Y.: Doubleday, 1969), p. 132.

The black liberation movement at this stage of its development can be interpreted in essentially the same terms as union struggles for higher wages and better working conditions. Concessions will come in proportion to the extent to which blacks and their white allies increase the costs of maintaining internal colonialism.[29] The relation between alternative costs is also important. If demands are very great, it may be rational from a narrow self-interest approach to repress the black movement. Ralph Abernathy attempts to show the loyalty of blacks to America and tries to awaken the white conscience, while the Black Panthers have called for black control of their community and liberation "by any means necessary." Token concessions to Abernathy and repression of the Panthers seems a sensible policy to some. As a general principle, Stephen Michelson suggests that "if whites are running a system in which overt black alienation must be kept to some acceptable minimum, then 'black power' is defined by the extent to which blacks can raise the cost of that minimum."[30] The operational concepts that then become relevant are to be found in bargaining models and game theory.

There is a small but growing number of blacks who see their struggle for autonomy and collective control over their communities as only the first step toward imposing new national priorities and forms of social and economic organization. Should black militants move beyond an essentially trade-union mentality, then they will be projecting the so-called two-stage revolutionary strategy: first the nationalist or racial struggle for power in the black community and then, in alliance with white groups, a class struggle for state power. Whether revolutionary or evolutionary strategies are followed, fundamental social change in this country can come only when enough whites join militant blacks in the struggle to end racial oppression. The job of whites who want such changes is twofold: to be objectively anti-racist in one's occupational role, and outside the workplace to be involved in basic education and political work.

[29] Huberman and Sweezy, "Reform and Revolution," pp. 8–9.
[30] Stephen Michelson, "On Income Differentials by Race: An Analysis and a Suggestion," *Conference Papers of the Union for Radical Political Economics* (Ann Arbor, Mich.: The Union for Radical Political Economics, 1968), p. 109.

The White Role

In recent years there has been an upsurge in advocacy activities, as evidenced in the increasing stress on the role of participant observer in social research, social commitment in the practice of law and medicine, and even advocate economics, as when the regressiveness of a tax "reform" is shown to hurt low-income people and to benefit the rich. Nowhere else has advocacy developed in and begun to take hold of a field and challenged its basic assumptions as in urban planning. Planners who until recently have assumed that they were being neutral technicians, only applying their tools of analysis as objectively as possible to serve a consensus view of the city, have begun to see how urban renewal, public housing, and the planning process in general tend to serve the interests of the construction and real estate industries but not those of the urban poor. Speaking of the advocate planner, Marshall Kaplan declares: "His role is to defend or prosecute the interests of his clients. The planning advocate links resource and strategy alternatives to objectives and joins issues at the request of his client when others' interpretation of facts overlooks, minimizes, or negatively affects his client's interests."[31]

The advocate planner seeks to rectify the social imbalance which follows from the lack of political power of the poor. He assumes that the "present distribution of public or private resources in American cities favors the haves, not the have-nots,"[32] and what is given the poor does not usually reflect their needs as the poor themselves view them. The ghetto dweller is excluded from decision-making and must accept the dictates of the dominant political groups. That their will is often thwarted results from so-called "value-free" research and management by governmental and quasi-public organizations. Advocate planners should be aware that "aggregation and analysis of facts involve, more often than not, the application of value systems."[33] The assumed values may not be those accepted by the black community. The advocate

[31] Marshall Kaplan, "Advocacy and the Urban Poor," *Journal of the American Institute of Planners*, March 1969, p. 97.
[32] *Ibid.*
[33] *Ibid.*

planner can help de-mystify the bureaucratic mode of operation and show its political content.

Most whites work in and with institutions which are objectively racist. Highway engineers can ask why highways are put through low-income rather than high-income neighborhoods. They can show the redistribution effects of government programs which sub-sidize suburban commuters and penalize ghetto residents. Whites who do not accept the confines of job roles which support a racist status quo will redefine the purpose of their jobs in relevant ways. Recent attempts by social workers to join striking welfare mothers in demanding more adequate living allowances is such an action. Cloward and Piven go still farther, suggesting that the way to change a bad system is to push it until it cannot function—to withhold payment if services are not being rendered adequately, and to mobilize people to claim benefits they are legally entitled to but which have been withheld.[34]

Two important things whites can do: First, they should support those blacks who are on the cutting edge of the struggle, the mili-tant groups that refuse to go slow and accept token reforms. Sec-ond, they should build a white movement for radical social change. Racism hurts whites in ways which must be made clear. Also, many liberal and radical whites must stop finding their only polit-ical fulfillment in supporting blacks and start to identify the causes of their own problems.

Finally, a word about the limits of the internal colony analogy and the possibilities of restructuring American social institutions. Black liberation in a meaningful sense cannot take place in a divided society. Separate can never be equal. At the same time, the nature of black oppression dictates that the struggle for justice—political and economic—involve blacks organizing blacks and whites supporting black struggles, but not attempting to lead them. This has been the message of the last half of the 1960s. The coming decade may witness meaningful cooperation based on mutual respect and common interest between blacks and whites,

[34] See Richard A. Cloward and Francis Fox Piven, "A Strategy to End Poverty," *The Nation*, May 2, 1966; reprinted in *Metropolis in Crisis*, ed. Jeffrey K. Hadden, Louis H. Masotti, and Calvin J. Larson (Itasca, Ill.: F. E. Peacock Publishing Co., 1967).

founded on a shared political perspective. At present, white worker racism stands in the way of the emergence of this alliance. The task is to find ways of breaking down this racism.

Many of what have passed as racial problems have a deeper dimension of a philosophical and moral character. How one man treats another and how a society uses its resources are certainly basic questions. The place of black people in America today raises questions of distributional justice. Satisfactory solutions to these problems, however, must be found beyond a series of political programs such as those Congress is now considering. It is also doubtful whether today's racial problems can be solved within the context of contemporary social institutions or under present national consensus on politically acceptable philosophies. Priorities are misdirected because they stress the values of a competitive, individualistic, profit-motivated society—which was an innovation in the time of Adam Smith, but now stands in the way of human progress.

The important group in the decade to come will be, for better or worse, the white working class. The questions blacks have raised concerning how society's resources should be distributed, the rights of all citizens to quality housing, jobs, and education—these are questions of profound importance to whites as well as blacks. There is a natural alliance of those excluded from the bounty of society—the blacks and other minorities, and the overtaxed white who has before him a life of continuous, boring, dreary, and alienating labor. They have a common cause in reorienting the economy and imposing new social relationships on society.

Index